I0051260

Virtual Business Franchise,
the billion dollar startup

Rudy Lewis, *Author*
Published by: NAHBB Publishing Company
Baltimore, Maryland

Virtual Business Franchise,
the billion dollar startup

Rudy Lewis, *Author*
Published by: NAHBB Publishing Company
Baltimore, Maryland

ISBN: 978-0-9890769-4-4

Outline

I. Introduction

Early Stage Franchising is a new field in the traditional franchise industry and home to the "Virtual Business Franchise", the highest level of franchising in use today, with 90% of its business functions performed electronically. This new method of franchising produces the billion dollar startup, the Next Big Thing! Thanks, to a small business investment bill that passed Congress and was signed into law by President Obama on April 5, 2012, as part of the Jobs Act. This new law made it possible for non-accredited investors to invest in early stage business ventures for the first times, since the 1930. Traditionally, you had to be an accredited investor with a net worth of $1 million dollars or more to invest directly in private ventures.

It is estimated than when this law is fully implement there will be more that 51 million new investors eligible to invest in private ventures. The biggest challenge these investors will face when entering the private equity market for the first time is deciding where and how to locate quality ventures to invest in. The key to success in early stage investing is finding the right business projects, during the embryonic stage of a new business idea.

The Early Stage Franchise Industry for startups was made possible by the establishment of the Early Stage Franchise Investment Exchange. This exchange form a major part of the private sector business infrastructure that connects small & medium enterprise owners that are seeking equity and venture capital to both accredited and non-accredited investors.

Early Stage Franchising provides a new business structure that starts at the embryonic stage of a business idea. The success of growing a franchise business can be found in statistic data with a success rate of more than 95% after five years, compared to the

90% failure rate of starting and growing a business using the traditional method of trial and error.

Early Stage Franchising is a private sector initiative that use special institutions to provide continues development and support to the franchise business system being offered. This is a predictable business structure that allows investors to easily follow the growth of the new ventures they invest in. When an Early Stage Franchise is first launched it is assigned a business development and support team to handle the constant changes it will face when entering the global marketplace.

A Virtual Business Franchise is developed in an authorized Franchise Incubator Accelerator and is planned from the start, unlike, the traditional startups that become successfully through trial and error. The Franchise Incubator Accelerator also converts certified business models into franchises in months instead of years. Concept Starter Enterprises include a Business Formation Incubator that specializes in the development of business formation models. It is also the exclusive provider of seed money projects that precedes the Virtual Business Franchise.

The Virtual Business Franchise is unique because of its global market reach the day it's launched. The Virtual Business Franchise has a Double Level Territory, one for virtual and another for physical locations. There are major differences between a Virtual Business Franchise and a traditional franchise. The traditional franchise uses physical landmark including land surveys to determine a business location, while the virtual business franchise use zip codes, email addresses, telephone numbers and GPS or the Global Positioning System to identify their customer base. When the territory purchased is large enough for additional franchise outlets, they can sell undeveloped franchise territories to early stage investors. A Virtual Level Territory maybe sold separately.

The Virtual Business Franchise combines the management structure of the chain store outlet with the multi-unit franchise marketing strategy. The chain store expansion strategy is used when offering an undeveloped territory to investors on the Early Stage Franchise Investment Exchange. This market system lets the owner sell both the physical and virtual franchise territory in the same agreement. This chain store expansion strategy is simply the multiplying of a successful outlet in a new market. The key to understanding early stage franchising is to understand the physical and virtual territory allocation of locations. When these two strategies are combined the Virtual Business Franchise can grow more rapidly in the new global marketplace.

A Virtual Business Franchise uses is a Dual-Unit Franchise System that maybe sold or leased as undeveloped franchise territory in parcels. The Dual-Unit Franchise System is a physical outlet that is surrounded by virtual franchise territories. The Dual-Unit Franchise System was first used in 2002, by CondoFran® an Affordable Condominium Apartment Conversion Service. It offered two systems, one for residential and another for commercial properties.

A Master Franchisee that buys a Multi-Unit Franchise as part of the purchase of a franchise territory may sell the Virtual Franchise Territory separately. They may also sell the virtual territory agreements without seeking permission from the Master Franchisee. What type of territory agreement used is determined by government agencies that oversee franchising rules in the country where it is registered? Before a Virtual Business Model or Franchise is sold the owner must have it certified by the Early Stage Franchise Association (ESFA).

In the future, 30% to 40% of all new business startups will use some form of Concept Funding which include: crowd funding donations, business formation grants, equity and/or venture capital. Concept Funding was first used after Title III of the Jobs Act was passed in 2012. Before, Concept Funding there was few financing options available to new entrepreneurs & existing small business owners that wanted to start or grow a business using equity capital.

We are living in the era of the "Billion Dollar Startup" and where a million dollars no longer make you rich, in this new era a million dollars merely defines a starting point. This era has changed the definition of what it takes to be wealthy. When government agencies began the lottery, their first prizes were in the range of $1 million dollars. Today, in order to get people interested they need near a half billion dollars jack pot.

Warren Buffett realized that in order to get people excited in this era, it would take a billion dollar bet. Warren Buffett, the American grand daddy of rich has a net worth $58 billion dollars, had fun with fellow Americans, by allowing them to bet online free to win $1 billion dollar, if they could correctly pick all the winning teams in the 66 team roster during the 2014, NCAA Basketball Tournament. No one won because the odd were against them however; we learned that it takes a billion dollars today for people to get excited.

Early Stage Franchising is the future of early investing, because it allows early investors to invest ventures from the embryonic stage of a new business idea to a full franchise system.

II.   **Early Stage Franchising**

Early Stage Franchising is a predictable business structure for investors that are new to private equity investing. The franchise business system provide investors with a known business structure to follow from a new business idea to a fully developed franchise. Early Stage Franchising includes a development process that is used to build a unique business system in a Franchise Incubator Accelerator in months instead of years.

Today, a Franchise Business Model starts in the embryonic stage of a new business idea. This lowers the cost of starting a business thereby, allowing ordinary people to invest in an new franchise models.

Globalization of Franchising

Early stage franchising is the outgrowth of the global impact on the private business structure for franchising. The globalization of franchising has changed the way Small & Medium size Enterprises (SMEs) start and grow in the 21st century. The globalization of franchising provides a worldwide standard for the Franchise Business Model which allows a Business Formation Model that's established in one country to be rapidly marketed in other countries. Globalization of franchising is at hand and it can provide unlimited opportunities to individuals involved in the private equity market for early stage startups. A globalized franchise business system offers the best protection for small investors that are new to investing in early stage startups, because this connects new franchise models directly to the United States franchise regulation process. Early Stage Franchising in now being used to turn national cities into global cities.

Multi-unit Franchising

Early Stage Franchising uses the multi-unit franchise marketing system to expand in authorized territories. When Early Stage Franchising is combined with the multi-unit franchise marketing system, it forms a new type of marketing structure that allows the franchise business system to keep pace with the speed of change in the new global marketplace. There are two distinct methods of establishing a multi-unit franchise system; one is for single units opened one at a time and another for dual-unit systems that can open more that in an authorized territory. The addition of the Dual-unit Franchise makes it more profitable than open one at a time. Even though single and multi-unit franchising offer two different methods of expansion, they both have proven track record of success.

A Master Franchisee that buys a multi-unit franchise marketing system as part of the purchase of a virtual territory may sell it separately from the physical franchise outlet. They may also sell their virtual territory agreements without seeking permission from the Franchisor. The type of selling agreement used is determined by government agencies that oversee franchising in the country where it is registered? The Franchise Business System provides a predictable infrastructure for small investors that are new to private equity investing.

Early Stage Startups

Early Stage Franchising offers a new business system that starts at the embryonic stage of a business idea. It provides entrepreneurs with uniform guidelines to follow, when entering business for the first time. The franchise business system offers the best protection for small investors that are new to investing in early stage startups and expanding business ventures. It also provides investors with a predictable business structure to easily follow the growth of the new ventures they invest in.

The success of growing a franchise business can be found in statistical data with a success rate of more than 95% after five years, compared to the 90% failure rate of starting and growing a business using traditional method of growth. When an Early Stage Franchise is launched it is assigned a business development & support team to handle the constant changes it will face when it enter the global marketplace.

Concept Starter Enterprise

ConceptStarter.Net provides the Business Formation Incubator services for global cities projects. This incubator system is part of a virtual incubator system that provides business & franchise conversion service in both domestic and foreign cities. Enrolled cities are awarded their own Concept Starter branches which will be attached to either www.conceptstarter.net or www.globalconceptstarter.net. This franchise business system provides a predictable business structure for small business owners and investors that invest in them. It also includes the Franchise Incubator Accelerator that converts certified business models into franchises.

Concept Starter Enterprises specializes in the development of virtual business franchises and is the exclusive providers of the special programs and services needed for the business formation and development models that precede the Virtual Business Franchise. Concept Starter is a major part of the Early Stage Franchise Development Structure that is attached to a "One World Business System" that can be implemented in all countries with Internet access. This allows the franchise business system to keep pace with the fast pace global.

Virtual Business Franchise

Early Stage Franchising is part of a newly established Franchise Formation Industry that's growing separate from the traditional franchise industry. Early Stage Franchising is a private sector initiative that uses special institutions to provide continuous development and support to the "Virtual Business Franchise", the highest form of franchising. Early Stage Franchising was made possible by a small business investment bill that passed Congress and was signed into law as: Title III of the of the 2012 Jobs Act. Early Stage Franchising offers excellent opportunities for both new entrepreneurs and small investors that are new to equity capital investing to participate in Early Stage Franchising.

The new law made it possible for new entrepreneurs and small business owners to raise equity capital directly from the general public. Importantly, those seek equity capital can by-pass traditional banks and other lending institutions and go directly to the people to raise equity capital. Early Stage Franchising will allow ordinary people to own and/or invest in a franchise brand of their choices. This law will change the way that small businesses start and grow in the United States and the world.

The Virtual Business Franchise has a Double Level Territory, one for virtual and another for physical locations. The key to understanding early stage franchising is to learn the difference in the method used to establish the physical and virtual locations, these territories maybe leased or sold separately. A Virtual Business Franchise is developed in an authorized Franchise Incubator Accelerator and is planned from the start. It is unlike, the traditional startups that maybe successfully through trial and error. The Virtual Business Franchise is unique because of its global market reach the day it is launched. Before a Virtual Business Model or Franchise is sold to non-accredited investors, the ownership of the venture must have the venture certified by the Early Stage Franchise Association (ESFA).

Early Stage Franchise Association

The Early Stage Franchise Association (ESFA) was established to oversee the formation and development process of Early Stage Franchise Models. A major goal of the Early Stage Franchise Association is to provide quality investment opportunities within the economic reach of ordinary people, especially those that lives in cities. This will also help economically empower people regardless of what country they live in. For example: the Early Stage Franchise Association has a Work-to-Own a Franchise Program that encourages individual employees and franchise owners to participate. This program is support by owners of franchise business system that are members of the ESFA. The ESFA also offer certification to affiliate institutions that work with early stage franchise owners seeking equity & venture capital using the Equity Capital Access Network. The Early Stage Franchise is part of the private sector institution that supports new business formation model from the embryonic stage of a business idea to a franchise business system. These franchise business models are developed exclusively in virtual business development incubators. However, not all franchise models that are built in a virtual incubator is certified.

Today, the National Association of Home Based Businesses (NAHBB), Micro-Business Enterprise Association (MBEA) and Early Stage Franchise Association (ESFA) officially use the term "FRAN" to describe a new franchise business trade group model. It was first used by a new Franchise Business Model in 2002 to describe the new Franchise Model "CondoFran" franchises a real estate Franchise Model that take month to develop rather than years. It is now used as a trademark for the condominium conversion franchise.

An Early Stage Franchise can sometime be recognize by names such as DentalFran, Business ModelFran, Lawn CareFran, SolarFran Energy and CondoFran our first official trademark. Many of these initial names will become trademarks for full-service franchises. Fran is a suffix or group of letters added to the end of a word or root, serving to form a new word or functioning as an inflectional ending. The suffix "Fran" is used to indicate an Early Stage Franchise Model. The suffix Fran maybe added to a business trade group for name that is assigned to an entity in the embryonic business stage. The key to success in early stage investing is finding the right business projects, during the embryonic stage of a new business idea. Early Stage Franchising provides a predictable business structure that both the business owners and the investor easily to follow.

The Early Stage Franchise Model is built on a development and support platform, so that it can be changed and updated rapidly when needed. These franchises are developed in two distinct stages, the first is the business model formation stage and the second is the franchise model development stage. The franchise business system provides a predictable business structure for small business owners that are new to ownership and investors that invest in them. The development process for a Virtual Business Model starts in a Concept Starter's authorized Franchise Incubator Accelerator.

Early Stage Franchise Classifications

The Early Stage Franchise Classification (ESFC) is a special Business Trade Group with a code guide number that is issued to business ventures that has met the requirements to apply for crowd funding donations or business formation grants using the Equity Capital Access Network. This classification is offered to entrepreneurs that have met the criteria for placing a business formation project on either ConceptStarter.Net or GlobalConceptStarter.Net. These numbers are stated in the following manner: Equity Capital SourceBank – ESFC: 20301.

There are new business trade groups being established worldwide that will use this classification system. Only the Early Stage Franchise Association may assign ESFC numbers to a new venture during the embryonic business stage of a new idea. The Early Stage Franchise Classification ESFC is a special Business Trade Group with a code guide number that is issued to business owners that have met the requirements to apply for business formation grants or crowd funding donations using the Equity Capital Access Network.

The following contain sample code guide numbers:

Early Stage Franchise Classifications

ESFC: 00911 - BUSINESS CONSULTING SERVICE
ESFC: 21022 - EQUITY STAKE EXCHANGE
ESFC: 24905 - EARLY STAGE BUSINESS FRANCHISE
ESFC: 25290 - BUSINESS FORMATION GRANT
ESFC: 33083 - BUSINESS FORMATION PROJECT
ESFC: 36721 - VIRTUAL BUSINESS FRANCHISE
ESFC: 44976 - FRANCHISE INCUBATOR ACCELERATOR
ESFC: 46097 - CONCEPT STARTER ENTERPRISE
ESFC: 55038 - BUSINESS FORMATION MODEL
ESFC: 56436 - VIRTUAL MARKETING STRATEGY
ESFC: 61378 - BUSINESS FORMATION INCUBATOR
ESFC: 68959 - VIRTUAL BUSINESS WEBSITE
ESFC: 78687 - BUSINESS TRADE GROUP
ESFC: 81082 - CONCEPT FUNDING
ESFC: 89934 - VIRTUAL BUSINESS INCUBATOR
ESFC: 96712 - MAIL ORDER SERVICE
ESFC: 98521 - CODE GUIDE NUMBER
ESFC: 98600 -GLOBAL CITIES PARTNERSHIP

Private Equity Capital Center

Early Stage Franchising is a private sector initiative that uses special institutions to provide continuous development and support for the franchise business system being offered; the "Private Equity Capital Center" is such an institution. The Private Equity Capital Centers are now being implemented however, prior to the selling of an independent franchise outlets in a select city, a Private Sector Business Infrastructure must be established for support. Each Private Equity Capital Center will have independent and major service providers attached. These independent service providers include professional and practical consultants as well as independent business enterprises that offer quality products and services needed by the different franchise business systems that use a center for develop and support.

The first fifteen (15) major U.S. cities have been selected for the implementation of a new Private Sector Business Infrastructure for early stage ventures. Early Stage Franchising is a private sector initiative that needs special institutions to provide continuous development and support for the franchise business system being offered; the Private Equity Capital Center is such an institution. The Private Equity Capital Center will be home to Early Stage Franchising, which is a private sector initiative that needs special institutions and professionals to provide continuing support for the new franchise being offered.

The Private Equity Capital Center is the hub for Franchise Incubator Accelerators that can also be sold as independent franchise outlets. Private Equity Capital Centers are being established in large U.S. cities to provide development and support services for new entrepreneurs and existing business owners seeking concept funding. These centers are used to provide new and existing business ventures with access to business development, equity and venture capital funding. Private Equity

Capital Centers will be located in local communities in a fully activated city. The Private Equity Capital Center for early stage start-ups has fully functioning concept funding platforms that finance ventures from the concept formation stage to a franchise system.

The Private Equity Capital Center is home to Early Stage Franchising, which is a private sector initiative that needs professionals to provide continuing support for the new franchise being offered. Private Equity Capital Centers are being established in large U.S. cities to provide development and support services for new entrepreneurs and existing business owners.

These centers are used to provide new and existing business ventures with access to business development, equity and venture capital funding. Private Equity Capital Centers are located in local communities in fully activated city. The Private Equity Capital Center for early stage startups has fully functioning concept funding platforms that finance ventures from the concept formation stage to a full franchise system.

These centers include Virtual Business Incubator as well as Business Formation Incubators such as: ConceptStarter.Net These incubators build business formation models for early stage ventures seeking equity and venture capital. They also provide development and certified business model converting services for new franchise business systems. The centers include virtual business formation and development training next generation entrepreneurs.

Early Stage Franchise Industry

In today's fast paced economy small business owners need access to business and support associates that can help them start and/or grow their business ventures. The world currently has two economies, one old, and the other new. The old economy depended heavily on debt financing by banks and other lending institutions. Small business owners operating in the new economy want rapid growth, therefore the prefer equity financing to start and build high growth companies. The current franchise business system is broken down into two parts, one for formation and the other for development. The first franchise business model, commonly known as the cookie cutter model, was made from the development stage of a business and famous by two fast food franchise outlets; McDonalds and Burger King.

The Early Stage Franchise Industry is the exclusive provider of programs and services for new entrepreneurs and existing business owners that want to build their businesses with concept funding. Concept funding includes; crowd funding donations, business formation grants, equity and venture capital. Early Stage Franchise Investment Exchanges uses business services professionals such as: business model plan writers, consultants, business developers, attorneys, accountants, and others that provide assistance and support to Small & Medium Enterprises (SMEs). The franchise investment exchange allows professionals & group users to acquire a license to use the Business Model Plan – Software Writing Platform.

III. Business Formation Platform

Concept Starter Enterprises build early stage business ventures for business owners and investors that are seeking quality equity investment projects. Concept Starter Enterprises offers a business and franchise development services that is used by early stage investors to help them locate suitable investment opportunities that start at the embryonic business stage.

ConceptStarter.Net is a Business Formation Incubator that starts the formation process during the early stage of a new business idea. Early stage business models are built exclusively in virtual business development incubators starting at the Embryonic Business Stage and progressing to a developed franchise system. This business formation structure allows a potential franchise model to originate in one country and rapidly expand to markets in other countries. However, the supply line for new enterprise(s) stays in the country of origin, thereby creating new manufacturing and distribution jobs in countries with a Private Sector Business Infrastructure.

In the past, equity capital investments were unavailable to ordinary people in the United States because of limits placed on them by states and federal laws that specify the amount of money an individual must have before they could invest. The old method of starting and growing a business was based on the Sea Turtle hatching theory of giving birth to hundreds in hopes that a few might survive to adulthood. In the modern world where there is no trade secrets new business concepts grown outside of a business structure are killed off by their competitors, before they reach the water's edge. The success of growing a business can be found in the statistics of the Franchise Business System with a success rate of more than 95% after five years, compared to the 90% failure rate of starting and growing a business using the traditional methods.

The new field of Business Concept Formation provides a more predictable way to grow a small business from the embryonic stage, thereby creating a more manageable business system for fast growth, once equity capital is received. During the business formation period an enrolled business owner may choose to raise funds in this period without issuing an equity stake in their company. However, new entrepreneurs will need funds to support their business formation models in its early stage of formation. This can be done through crowd funding donations and business formation grants. Business Concept Formation is a necessary first step for new entrepreneurs and business owners with existing ventures seeking equity capital. Concept funding is a better option for an owner with business ventures that is seeking equity capital for the first time.

A small business owner that use ConceptStarter.Net may elect to accept equity capital at the time the Business Formation Model is complete. The owner must also accept complete management oversight over the project in the business formation and franchise model development stages for at least three funding cycles.

Business Formation Incubator

ConceptStarter.Net is a Business Formation Incubator that builds business formation models that want to seek equity capital when the model is certified. ConceptStarter.Net has a development module inside the Franchise Incubator Accelerator which converts certified business models into franchises in months instead of years. ConceptStarter.Net provides business formation platforms for early stage start-ups that are seeking Concept Funding that including: crowd funding donations, business formation grants, and/or equity and venture capital. Business formation projects that are offered on ConceptStarter.Net may accept crowd funding donations or business formation grants. These grants are used as seed capital to build the business structure and certify its readiness as a Business Formation Model to receive equity capital funding from investors.

ConceptStarter.Net is a Business Formation Incubator for the embryonic stage of new business ideas. It provides business formation platforms for early stage start-ups that are seeking crowd funding donations, business formation grants, and equity investment capital. ConceptStarter.Net is part of a virtual business incubator system with pre-selected consultants and business developers attached to service the business needs of the owner of a selected project.

ConceptStarter.Net accepts business formation grants awarded as seed money in the embryonic stage of a new business idea. These grants are contributed by Donor Contributors for ventures that need a Business Formation Model to attract equity and/or venture capital to selected projects. Once the new crowd funding law is fully implemented in 2016, it will be hard for small investors that are new to equity investing to find quality ventures to invest in without guidance. The Early Stage Franchise Business System is broken into two major development periods, the first is the Concept Formation Stage, and the second is called the Model Development Stage.

The first level contributor may purchase the entire equity stake allotment; usually around (5%) five percent of the project being offered, then the next levels are emailed every 24hours, until all members have been notified or until the remaining allotted stakes are sold. If at the end of this process all shares that were made available are not sold, the owner(s) has the sole option to sell the remaining shares to other investors and/or the general public. There is a major different between buying a stake in a new company and buying stock in a large corporation. When you invest in early stage start-ups, you will get a stake in the company. If you wait until the company stock is sold on a public stock exchange, there could be major difference in the value of your purchase.

Concept Funding is an early-stage funding source that allows operational flexibility over the venture in the short term. Crowding funding includes donations and business formation grants that are used as seed capital. Business formation grants can provide an option that let a Donor Contributor participate in the growth of a company where they make their initial contribution. In the concept formation stage a company may sell equity shares to a single investor or a group of investors for the total amount of the funds needed. Concept funding investors are not buying stock in a company; instead they are buying a stake in the company they select. A single investor has the option to join an existing investment group or make the full investment needed.

Concept Starter is a major part of the business organization that is establishing the Small & Medium Enterprise (SME) Investment Exchange in major U.S. Cities. These exchanges can also be accessed through two websites: EquityStakeExchange.Com & the FranchiseStockExchange.Com, thereby, making them capable of being accessible from the Internet in any country that allows the worldwide web.

Virtual Formation Services
ConceptStarter.Net is also part of the Equity Access Capital Network which offers development and support platforms for business owners that are seeking equity and venture capital. ConceptStarter.Net is a virtual incubator module inside the Franchise Incubator Accelerator that provides new entrepreneurs and others with assistance from concept formation to franchise model development. The Franchise Incubator Accelerator is part of a company support network which must be established prior to independent franchise outlets being sold to the public. This assures the long term success of franchisees in local markets.

The mission of ConceptStarter.Net is to provide virtual formation services to new business ventures for owners seeking access to Concept Funding. Business formation grants are an alternative to crowd funding donations. A business formation grant is awarded to entrepreneurs as seed money to establish a Business Formation Model for a new business idea. These grants are awarded by donor contributors that award grants as individuals and groups. They contribute seed money in the form of grants to the owner of a new business venture. These grants are given to specific ventures in exchange for an Investment Participation Level (IPL) and the exclusive option to buy a stake in a company, if and when the owner is ready to accept equity capital investments.

A Business Formation Grant is awarded to entrepreneurs that are establishing a Business Formation Model. These grants are contributed by donor contributors for ventures that need a Business Formation Model to attract equity and/or venture capital. Unlike crowd funding donations where you get nothing for their donation, a Donor Contributor that awards a formation grant to a project is assigned an Investment Participation Level based on the amount they provide to the project receiving the grant. Business formation grants are awarded as seed money in the embryonic stage of a new business idea. These grants are given to specific ventures in exchange for an Investment Participation Level and the first option to buy an equity stake in the company when and if the new company is ready to accept equity investors. Some offer business formation grants to new ventures, with special emphasis on the ones starting in the contributor's community.

Once, the model is built and certified for its readiness to receive equity capital funding, the contributors that provide the grants will receive first option to invest if and when the owner is ready to accept equity capital. During this business development stage, independent consultants provide assistance before the structure is actually established. Only business formation models with future franchise business systems maybe accepted for equity funding.

Business Formation Period

The Business Formation Period has become one of the most lucrative period in early stage investing. Early Stage Investors (ESIs) are now investing millions of dollars in the embryonic stage of a new business idea. It has been reported that these investors are investing from $1 to $10 million dollars in business ventures during the Business Formation Period.

In 2012, the Equity Capital Access Network set aside the Business Formation Period to raise seed capital and to provide ordinary people with a chance to get involve in early stage investing as donor contributors. The chance to invest in early stage startups have been all but wiped out today, because of the high price evaluations for new business ventures. We estimate that since, Title III of the Jobs Act was signed into law in April 2012 the prices of startups have increased more than 5,000 percent. This will make it more difficult for small investors to find quality ventures to invest in without guidance. Now even angle investors are being priced out of the startup market, while mutual and retirement fund managers are now entering the Early Stage Startup Market. It is too soon to determine how these new funds will affect the growth and quality of small businesses over the long term.

Today, there are major gaps between the times a business concept is conceived, and when the product and/or service reaches the marketplace ready to be sold. The lack of a clear path to growth for small business owners in the United States can be traced to the beginning of the country, when wealthy landowners owned and controlled all properties and business activities. The establishment of a development Infrastructure, in local communities, will go a long way to assist entrepreneurs that need equity and venture capital to start and grow small business enterprises. The world's major stock exchanges serve as the funding infrastructure for major corporations. These exchanges provide big businesses with a place to sell stock and gain access to an unlimited amount of capital to grow and expand their companies.

Franchise Incubator Accelerator provides new entrepreneurs and others with assistance in business formation and access to Concept Funding including; crowd funding donations, business formation grants, equity and venture capital. There are two types of concept funding projects accepted by ConceptStarter.Net: the first is capital for business formation, and the second is equity capital for early stage start-ups with a viable Business Model Plan.

The establishment of a Private Sector Business Infrastructure for small business owners will help new entrepreneurs and others take the guess work out of raising equity and venture capital. They can use the Dot-Com Business Incubator's Business Model Plan Template to create a custom document for their business enterprises that can be presented to a new class of angel investors and unaccredited investors. These venture capital sources use the Business Model Plan exclusively to evaluate investment opportunities before they invest.

Starting a small business venture today without aiming it at a large growth fund, is not a good business practice in light of the fast pace global marketplace and the widespread use of the Internet by large corporations. Big business is not going it alone today; they're moving faster than even to establish mega business enterprises using the Internet because they don't fear monopoly laws in a single country, because when using the Internet there are no laws against size. In order for small businesses to start and grow in the face of this competition they must create a parallel business infrastructure that will allow them to continue to grow!

Embryonic Business Stage

ConceptStarter.Net is a Business Formation Incubator for the embryonic stage of new business ideas. It provides business formation platforms for early stage start-ups that are seeking crowd funding donations, business formation grants and equity investment capital. ConceptStarter.Net is part of a virtual business incubator system with pre-selected consultants and business developers attached to service the needs of the business owner.

A Business development team will be assembled with the needs of the business enterprise being developed in mind. Team members can provide assistance to the venture before and after funding. This help assures an investor that a dependable business team will always be in place to guide the business venture forward, regardless of the lack of business ability and skills of the original owner. Since new businesses start with a "Business Model Plan" that is a development and growth document that interchangeable so that all business development teams may use it, this allows teams to be located in any area of a country.

Business Formation Grants

Concept Starter Enterprises has established a new way to allow small investors to gain access to quality investment ventures. A new entrepreneur may choose to raise funds during the formation period of a new business venture without issuing an equity stake in their company; this is done through business formation grants, a viable alternative to crowd funding donations. Business formation grants are awarded to a specific venture for an option to buy a stake in the company if and when the owner is ready to accept equity capital. The Donor Contributor that awards such grants will receive the first option to invest when the owner sells an equity stake in their company. A startup venture requires several rounds of financing, before it can generate sufficient cash flow to finance its own operations.

Donor Contributor

Business formation grants are awarded by individuals and business groups as seed money for new business ventures. Donor contributors that ward such grants will get the first option to invest if and when the owner sells an equity stake in their company. A Donor Contributor that subscribe to Concept Starter membership program will get the first option to sell their stake at the 3rd funding cycle, when the original owner(s) shares are most likely to be diluted. Therefore, all future fund raised will be acquired from private sector investors worldwide.

The Concept Starter Enterprises establishes Private Equity Capital Centers in large cities both domestic and foreign cities. A major goal of this type of funding program is to connect large U.S. cities with new entrepreneurs in developing nations. This will let franchise ideas be discovered in one country to be converted into a franchise business system and spread to other countries enrolled in the network. The supply line that services the new enterprise(s) will stay in the country of origin, thereby creating manufacturing jobs.

All potential franchise business systems found abroad will be developed and maintained exclusively in the United States, in accordance with federal and state laws where they are authorized. This will allow the franchise model to maintain their creditability as a viable option with a quality franchise business system.

Grant Award Agreement

Whereas: the Donor Contributor wishes to benefit from an affiliation with Concept Starter Enterprises and their business model development services. Now, therefore, in consideration of the premises and the mutual covenants herein contained, the parties hereto agree as follows:

The Donor Contributor understands that the project owner may choose to raise funds in the formation period of a new business venture without issuing an equity stake in their company. This is done through Crowd Funding Donations and Business Formation Grants. The Donor Contributor further understands that the Business Formation Grant is awarded to the project that needs a Business Formation Model to attract equity and/or venture capital, in their next round of funding. Once the model is certified for its readiness to receive equity capital funding, the Donor Contributor will receive first option to invest when the owner of the project is ready to accept equity funding. This grant is given to a specific venture in the name that appears in this agreement as the "Business Formation Project". The grant is awarded in exchange for an Investment Participate Level and the exclusive option to buy a stake in the company if and when the owner is ready to accept equity capital investments.

This Business Formation Grant or Crowd Funding Donation will be used as seed funds to build a Business Formation Model for the company, product prototype, trade/mark(s) to generate sufficient investor interest for successive financing rounds. The Donor Contributor further understands that the funds may be used for the following: business research, trademarks, logos, website development, business consulting, business development services, salaries, commissions, selling strategies, direct mail, brochures, marketing, customer evaluations & surveys, target marketing & feasibility studies, trade shows, travels, lodging and other necessary activities that will result in the development of a viable Business Formation Model. The Early Stage Franchise Business System is broken into two major development periods, the first is the Concept Formation Stage, and the second is the franchise Model Development Stage.

Electronic Wall Street is a business formation and franchise development models showcase for listings posted on the Equity Stake Exchange and the Franchise Stock Exchange. Electronic Wall Street is made possible because of a series of certified business models and franchise listings.

Business Formation Model

A business owner may choose to raise funds in the formation period of a new business venture without issuing an equity stake in their company or partnership. Today, the formation portion of a new venture is done through the use of crowding funding donations and business formation grants. When you award a business owner with a Business Formation Grant, you will get an option to invest in the company when the owner sells equity stakes in the company.

The small business investment provision that was signed into law, created the need for a new type of investor, the "Donor Contributor". A Donor Contributor that provides business formation grants is the first to be notified when the Business Formation Project they selected is ready to receive equity funding. Many of the people that make grant contributions are new to equity investing. They award a grant to a project to slow the business development process for themselves, so they can understand the growth of an embryonic stage of a new idea.

The private investor's role is being redefined by the government as crowd funding donors and small equity investors reach the new investment marketplace. The law provision called Title II of the Jobs Act, has even defined the investment options for donations and equity investments. The new law makes it possible for small investors to invest in new business ventures. A Donor Contributor that provides business formation grants is the first to be notified when the Business Formation Project they selected is ready to receive equity funding.

Crowd Funding Donations

Crowd funding donations has been around for a long time. It was made famous as a primary source of funding to launch new projects in theaters, such as plays and movies. In the past crowd funding campaigns provided donations with no obligation to pay it back even when the project became successful. Those who make crowd funding donations may receive special considerations in the form of gifts, tickets, products and sometimes services from the enterprise being funded, but no investment considerations.

Crowd funding donations is a very old idea that is new again and offered by websites such as: Kickstarter and Indiegogo, which cater to artists, inventors, filmmakers, game publishers, video producers and others. But now the challenge is to extend these models to all kinds of business enterprises. The goal of crowd funding will give kitchen table investors the ability to buy into a much broader range of opportunities, and will give start-ups access to a whole new pool of capital, the money sitting in every American's checking or savings account. In just a few short years crowd funding websites has evolved into a separate funding class from its roots in the field of donations for such projects as: movies, games, theater plays and book publishing projects.

Crowd financing is used to describe a group of people who pool their resources to support projects initiated by others. Crowd funding donations occur for a wide variety of purposes including; disaster relief, writing & music projects, support of artists by fans, political campaigns, video productions, and many other start-up projects.

Technology has change the meaning of crowd funding, with people on the Internet raising thousands of dollars and a few projects millions. A technology company name Pebble, an electronic paper watch company, raises more than $3 million dollars in less than a week on Kickstarter, a crowd funding website, even though the owner only asked for $100,000 initially. Update: During its month-long crowdfunding campaign, ending in March of 2015, MarrkPebble Time shattered two Kickstarter records. The Pebble Time is second generation smartwatch with week-long battery life. It broke its first record on its first day, when it became the fastest project to raise $1 million in 49 minutes. A week later, it became the most-funded campaign in Kickstarter's history after receiving more than $13.3 million in pledges, besting Coolest Cooler, the previous record holder.

In total, Pebble has raised $20,336,930 from 78,463 people. Pebble's initial goal to raise $500,000 was too easy of a hurdle. Each watch was sold for $159 to early backers, and $179 for just about everyone else. Three years ago, Pebble raised more than $10 million from 69,000 people on the crowd funding site for its first product, the original Pebble Watch. The company's goal at the time was also an easy target $100,000. *Source: CNNMoney 2015* Carmageddon a UK based company raised more than $625,000 in June of 2012. A video production company with a project called; Double Fine Adventure, raised $3.3 million. There are also successful projects such as Stack that raise more than $17,921 in donations or double what they asked for from more than 1,113 people acting as crowd funders.

KickStarter.Com an American crowd funding website raised $480 million dollars in 2013 and three months later it reached $1 billion dollar. In a new business venture crowding funding includes donations and business formation grants may be used as seed capital to start a new business venture. Crowd funding websites has change the meaning of crowd funding, with people on the Internet raising thousands of dollars, and a few projects millions.

Concept Funding raised during the business formation and early stage growth of a new business venture provide the owner with operational flexibility over the venture in the short term. Once, the business model is complete and a value is established, the Donor Contributor will get a priority investment level assigned to them. Equity shares are made available to the Contributor and others during the concept formation stage of a new business venture.

ConceptStarter.Net™ is a new high-tech website that provides access to both crowd and equity funding projects. It will replace the needs for crowd funding websites only, because it provides crowd funding donations, business formation grants and equity funding projects. ConceptStarter.Net is in a class by itself and will force websites, like Kickstarter, to change their business message, if they are to offer access to equity funding to comply with the small business investment provision signed into law by the Jobs Act.

A company can raise concept funds by using donors without issuing an equity stake in their company. Once a company accepts business formation grants, equity shares may not be sold until a partnership is formed, the company is sold, mortgaged, transferred, or when an actual value is assigned to the business venture by an outside source. There are two types of concept funding projects accepted by ConceptStarter.Net, they are: 1) *Concept Funding for business formation and 2) investment capital for early stage start-ups.*

Crowd Funding Law
The new Crowd Funding Law will make it possible to fund new start-up ventures in the concept formation stage. Concept Funding is capital raised during the business formation period and early

stage growth of a new business venture. There are two types of concept funding projects that qualify; the first is capital raised for business formation, and the second is equity capital raised for early stage start-ups with a Certified Business Model Plan. This Private Equity Market for early stage start-ups has the potential to grow into one of largest investment markets in the world and you are witnessing its beginnings.

The western style free market system is now the world's leading business and trade structure in the world and today most independent countries prefer it. All industrialized countries are using the Free Enterprise System or is currently implementing some form of free market economics. This private entrepreneurial system can assist small businesses owners survive the shift to the new global economy system. However, access to small business ownership is being restricted and priced out of the reach of ordinary people that don't cater to a niche market.

Traditional entrepreneurs that started businesses exist on less that 25% of what a Certified Business Model can generate. Business models that are third party verified can be more profitable than their counterparts that are grown with traditional methods. Traditional business models have no business development team in place to help them find hidden opportunities in their business trade groups. Traditionally, the Private Equity Industry's most common investment strategies consist of leveraged buyouts using venture capital, growth capital, distressed investments and mezzanine capital funding. This type of private equity financing is an asset-class that consists of an equity stake in an operating company that is not traded on a public stock exchange.

Bloomberg Business Week has called private equity a rebranding of leveraged buyout firms after 1980s. In a typical leveraged buyout transaction a private equity firm buys majority control of an existing or mature firm. This is distinct from a venture using capital growth capital investment in which the investors (typically venture capital firms or angel investors) invest in early stage or emerging companies. At the end of 2010, the private equity market had a totaled of $2.4 trillion dollars under management and more than $1 trillion available for investments, which was 40% of overall assets under management.

The newly enhanced equity capital access and investment rules for unaccredited investors were recently enacted in the United States, thereby, removing equity capital access barriers for new entrepreneurs and small business owners that had been in place for more than 80 years. This law also made it possible to globalize franchising thereby allows ordinary people to own a global franchise brand of their choice. In the future, there will be few high paying jobs for people seeking long term employment. Likewise, fixed salary positions are fast becoming a thing of the past. Purchasing a Franchise Business System that offers the potential income level you seek will be the only alternative for left many seeking income security.

Public & Private Grants
A business funding grant is an award of financial assistance in the form of money by government, private individuals, and organizations with no obligation to pay the funds back. The offer of a small business grants is a monetary gift bestowed usually on new entrepreneurs that want to start their own business ventures. While the federal government doesn't offer many direct business grants, some states and private groups have endowments available to grant applicants. Private and philanthropic organizations also offer a variety of grants.

Generally, most people who are looking for money to start or expand a small business have a much better chance of finding and getting a small business loan than a small business grant. Whichever type of funding you decide to pursue, conduct research on what type of grant you want to pursue, this section will help you streamline your search for the money your small business enterprise needs. There are ways to obtain small business grants, if you fit certain criteria. You may also be able to qualify for a specialized small business grant through state agencies. Small business grants are funds provided to start or expand a qualifying small-to-medium-size enterprise that do not need to be paid back. Another reason small business grants are difficult to get is that they usually have very stringent requirements that applicants must meet.

Small business grants are often only available to individuals of a certain demographic who reside in a particular place, as well as being tied to a particular condition of business or certain industry. The first step is to conducting research and finding a grant that your company might qualify for.

The Wild West business philosophy of "if the thing don't kill you, you will grow strong", is being replaced with business formation services and concept funding for start-ups. Today, we grow plants in indoor nurseries and hatch chickens from eggs in hatcheries. The old philosophy of starting a business by trial and error, has given way to a new virtual incubator development strategies. The combination of these two new business formation tools will provide a more predictable way to grow a small business venture from an embryonic or idea stage into a more manageable business system.

Minority Business Grants
If you are a minority business owner, you might take advantage of minority small business grants such as a woman or part of any ethnic group that is considered a minority, you have a lot of options available. Federal small business grants for women and other minorities are the government's way of trying to level the playing field when it comes to business. There are hundreds of

websites online that link to beneficial grants for your business as long as you qualify.

The Minority Business Development Agency (MBDA) provides a page of state grant resources, such as how and where to possibly obtain a grant through your state. The MBDA exists to provide resources for minority business owners, from possible grant leads and links to relevant conferences to general advice. Before applying for grants for minority business owners, get registered at Grants.gov. This will get you access to lists of available grants that are constantly updated.

The U.S. Small Business Administration lists resources for each state so you can check out requirements to get a grant or other financial possibilities. There are many types of grants that exist to help different kind of businesses or to help with specific business needs. Some grants are for women or minority-owned small businesses, while other grants may help a company become handicap accessible. Small businesses focusing on education or science may receive grants because of contributions to society.

Business Innovation Research

There are grants include the Small Business Innovation Research program and the Small Business Technology Transfer program. Two kinds of grants are endowed by the federal research and development government and granted specifically to small businesses engaged in scientific research and development. To qualify for these small business grants, companies must meet federal goals and develop products with a high level of potential commercialization. Other types of grants include venture capital and low-interest loans. Generally, grants offer otherwise unattainable financial opportunities to small businesses and small business owners.

Government programs such as Small Business Innovation Research (SBIR) and Small Business Technology Transfer (STTR) give a certain percentage of research and development funds to eligible small businesses. In addition, if your company falls into a specific niche, such as industries that deal with housing, education, energy, transportation, or security, the government might have a grant for you. Perform research within your company that the government might be interested in, could give you a shot at a federal grant. SBIR.gov has a page of possible funding opportunities for your small business if you choose to participate in research, and includes a list of solicitation dates for funding.

Independent & Major Service Providers
The Private Sector Business Infrastructure includes Independent & Major Service that offers quality products and services that can be used by franchisees. Qualified service providers are invited to bid before outside bids are sought! These service provider teams include; financial brokers & agents, lawyers, marketing & management firms, and other business trade group members. The first steps in determining where and how a new provider might fit in the network's Priority Bid Right Program, which gives special marketing rights to members on develop and marketing teams.

Private Equity Capital Centers are now being established, however prior to the selling of independent franchise outlets a support, infrastructure must be implemented. Each Private Equity Capital Center will have Independent and major service providers attached. These Independent & Major Service Providers include professional and practical consultants as well as independent business enterprises that offer quality products and services needed by the different franchise business systems that use a center for develop and support.

Business Concept Formation

Many times, during the business formation stage, a new business may not have a name or logo. This is the embryonic stage of a new business idea. Business formation projects are funded by crowd funding donations, business formation grants and equity capital investments. The small business investment provision signed into law by President Obama made it possible for business owners and new entrepreneurs to raise capital directly from the general public.

Early stage franchising is a private sector initiative that needs special institutions to provide continued development support to the franchise system being offered. When an Early Stage Franchise is first launched, it is assigned a business development and support team to handle the constant changes it will face when entering the new global marketplace. The success of growing a franchise business system can be found in statistic data with a success rate of more than 95% after five years, compared to the 90% failure rate of starting and growing a business using the traditional method of trial and error.

The new field of Business Concept Formation provides a more predictable way to grow a small business venture from the embryonic stage of a new business idea, thereby creating a more manageable business system for fast growth, once equity capital is received. In the concept formation period a company may sell an equity stake to a single investor or a group of investors for the total amount of funds needed. Concept funding investors are not buying stock in a company; instead they are buying a stake in the company they select. A single investor has the option to join an existing investment group or make the full investment needed themselves.

Business Trade Group

In the field of Business Concept Formation there are new business trade groups that are used to recognize an embryonic stage of a new business idea. Small business enterprises that successfully complete the business formation stage will be assigned a Business Trade Group (BTG) with a special code guide number from one of the two associations that are authorized exclusively to issue these numbers. The National Association of Home Based Businesses (NAHBB) and the Micro Business Enterprise Association (MBEA) assigned these code guide numbers to new business trade groups. The Home Business Identity Classification (HBIC) assigned "Business Concept Formation – HBIC: 64621" and the Micro Business Trade Classification (MBTC) is "Business Concept Formation – MBTC: 64621".

All new business ventures that qualify for business formation service will be assigned a Business Trade Group to be listed under a code guide number that identifies the business industry. The Business Formation Stage is a necessary step for entrepreneurs with new business ideas that are seeking equity capital.

During the business formation period a business owner may choose to raise funds in the formation period of a new business enterprise without issuing an equity stake in their company. This is done through crowding funding donations and business formation grants. When you award a business owner with a Business Formation Grant, you will get an option to invest in the company when the owner sells equity shares to their company.

The business funding grant is an award for financial assistance in the form of money by government, private individuals, and organizations with no obligation to pay the funds back. The offer of a small business grants is a monetary gift bestowed on new entrepreneurs that want to start their own business ventures. An entrepreneur that is qualified to use ConceptStarter.Net to raise concept funds can do so without issuing an equity stake in their company. Equity shares are not issued until a partnership is formed, the company is sold, mortgaged, transferred or when an actual value is assigned to the business venture by an outside source.

A Business Formation Grant is awarded to an entrepreneur that is establishing a Business Formation Model; once the model is built and certified for its readiness to receive equity capital funding. Contributors that provide the grant will receive first option to invest when the owner is ready to accept equity capital. During this business development stage, independent consultants provide assistance before the structure is actually established. Only certified business models and franchise business systems are accepted for equity funding. The embryonic stage of business ventures built in virtual business incubators by experienced business developers and consultants before they reach the marketplace.

Support Organization
In the past, traditional venture capitalists wanted companies that had been in business for at least seven years. Therefore, Start-ups were rarely funded unless they were in high tech or biological research fields. Equity funding sources for low tech and start-up business ventures were limited because they were not structured for equity capital financing. Today, however, all that is about to change with the introduction of new investment scoring systems and certified business models that can be converted into a franchises in months instead of years.

An entrepreneur that is qualified to use ConceptStarter.Net to raise concept funds can use business formation grants without issuing an equity stake in their company. Equity shares are not issued until a partnership is formed, the company is sold, mortgaged, transferred or when an actual value is assigned to the business venture by an outside source. There are two types of concept funding projects accepted by ConceptStarter.Net are: 1) *Concept funding for business formation and 2) investment capital for early stage start-ups.* Many times, during the business formation stage, a new business may not have a name or logo. This is the embryonic stage of a business idea. Business formation projects are funded by crowd funding donations, business formation grants and later by equity capital investments.

Entrepreneurs, that want to start a company and move quickly to raising equity and venture capital funds for growth, can turn to ConceptStarter.Net. They can use this Business Formation Platform to raise funds for formation on the Electronic Wall Street Showcase for fast growth. Concept Funding is capital raised during the business formation stage of a new business venture. There are two types of concept funding accepted for these types of projects: the first is capital raised for business formation, and the second is equity capital raised for early stage start-ups with certified business model plans.

Thanks, to the establishment of the Private Equity Industry for startups, the embryonic stage of new business ventures will be recognized by experienced business developers and consultants before they reach the actual marketplace. This early stage growth period was established exclusively for business ventures that need equity capital to facilitate their transitions to a Business Development Model. In the concept formation stage a company may sell equity shares to a single investor or a group of investors for the total amount of the funds needed.

Concept Formation Investor
Concept Funding is part of the Equity Access Capital Network which offers development and support platforms to business owners seeking equity and venture capital. Concept formation investors are not buying stock in the formation project they select, instead they participating in the build process because many of the shares to a project may be sold out quickly, for certified business models and franchises.

The reality for new entrepreneurs to raise capital has change forever; caused by private investors and venture capital firms that will let them name their prices for early stage ventures, they started. In the future these business ventures will be sold like commodities and shares will be carved up and sold to the highest bidder. When people use to think start-ups they thought Silicon Valley, CA., Austin TX., or Boston MA. But investors and entrepreneurs say a new group of startup cities are emerging, some in unlikely places such as: Boulder, Colorado stand out, it has a proven startup development program. Entrepreneurs there say the city, which borders the Rocky Mountains just northwest of Denver, has all the benefits of Silicon Valley. Fewer than 300,000 people live near Boulder, but it draws more venture capital than cities many times its size. Many refer to it as the best in the country and the program claims strong stats to back that up. Since it began in 2007, the program has helped 65 startups reaching $115 million in funding. All but 8 were acquired by other companies or remain active. Future founders of high growth investment projects will not be an active part of the ventures they once owned.

IV.   Private Equity Industry

The history of the Private Equity Industry in the United States can be traced to the late 1800s and the Union Pacific Railroad, the United States first transcontinental railroad. It had been run by a corrupt management that ran the railroad badly and it collapsed into bankruptcy in 1893. Edward H. Harriman with financial investments firm Abraham Kuhn and Solomon Loeb took over the company and turned it into one of the most profitable companies in American history. This made E.H. Harriman one of the richest men in the country at the time while greatly increasing the profits of Kuhn and Loeb his investment partners. The Investment bank was founded 1867 by Abraham Kuhn and Solomon Loeb merged with Lehman Brothers in 1977. *(Lehman Brothers filed for bankruptcy in 2008.)*

John Pierpont Morgan was another American financier and banker who dominated corporate finance. In 1901 J.P. Morgan & Co. handled what is arguably the world's first leveraged buyout. Morgan bought out the Carnegie Steel Corporation for $480 million. (J.P. Morgan congratulated Andrew Carnegie on becoming "the richest man in the world" when Carnegie accepted the deal.) The corporation's assets were merged with those of other companies and Morgan formed the largest company the world had ever seen, United States Steel, capitalized at a staggering $1.4 billion. (For spending comparison, the federal government spent $524 million that year.) Carnegie and his partners were paid in bonds of the new corporation that were floated by Morgan.

The venture capital fund makes money by owning equity in the companies it invests in which usually have a business model in high technology industries. The typical venture capital investment occurs after the seed funding round as growth capital funding. Venture capital may be provided by wealthy individual investors, professionally managed investment funds. Whereas banks tend to focus on companies' past performance when evaluating them for loans, venture capital firms tend to focus instead on their future potential. As a result, venture capital organizations will examine the features of a business's product, the size of its markets, and its projected earnings.

The thirty-five-year period between 1946 and the end of the 1970s were characterized by relatively small volumes of private equity investment, rudimentary firm organizations and limited awareness of and familiarity with the Private Equity Industry. Within the broader Private Equity Industry, two distinct sub-industries, leveraged buyouts and venture capital experienced growth along parallel although inter-related tracks. The early history of private equity relates to one of the major periods in the history of private equity and venture capital.

Modern Era Financing

It was in the 1960s that the common form of private equity funds, still in use today, emerged. Private equity firms organized limited partnerships to hold investments in which professional funding managers served as general partner and investors who put up the capital are passive and limited partners.

The modern era of private equity industry in the United States can be traced to 1946 with the formation of the first venture capital firms. Venture capital is a type of equity investment usually made in rapidly growing companies or start-ups that can show through their business plans that they have strong growth potential.

Since 1946, there have been three boom and bust cycles. During the 1960s and 1970s, venture capital firms focused their investment activity primarily on starting and expanding companies. More often than not, these companies were exploiting breakthroughs in electronic, medical or data-processing technology. As a result, venture capital came to be almost synonymous with technology finance. The compensation structure, still in use today, also emerged with limited partners paying an annual management fee and a carried interest typically representing up to 20% of the profits of the partnership.

It is commonly known, that the first venture-backed startup was Fairchild Semiconductor that produced the first commercially practicable integrated circuit, and was venture capital funded in 1959 by what would later become Venrock Associates. Venrock was founded in 1969 by Laurance S. Rockefeller, a venture capitalist, financier, philanthropist, a major conservationist, and a prominent third-generation member of the Rockefeller family. He and other Rockefeller children were exposed to venture capital investments early.

In its early years through roughly the year 2000, the history of the private equity and venture capital asset classes is best described through a narrative of developments in the United States as private equity. Other countries, including those in Europe, lagged behind the United American Private Equity Industry. With the second private equity boom in the mid-1990s and liberalization of regulation for institutional investors in Europe, the emergence of a mature European private equity market has occurred.

The first boom and bust cycle, from 1982 through 1993, was characterized by the dramatic surge in leveraged buyout activity financed by junk bonds and culminating in the massive buyout of RJR Nabisco before the near collapse of the leveraged buyout industry in the late 1980s and early 1990s. While the private-equity firm is new, venture capital, growth capital, distressed situations, leveraged buyouts and others are as old as capitalism itself. The term remains a loose one, since many companies not thought of as private-equity firms such as Warren Buffett's

Berkshire Hathaway, use the same financial investment techniques as traditional venture capital firms.

Venture Capital Firms

The Private Equity Industry in the modern era can be traced from 1946 with the formation of venture capital firms. Venture capital is a type of equity investment usually made in rapidly growing companies that require a lot of capital or start-up companies that show they have strong growth potential that can be shown through their business plan. The venture capital fund makes money by owning equity in the companies it invests in, which usually have a business model in high technology industries. The typical venture capital investment occurs after the seed funding round is completed and the venture needs additional funding to grow.

Venture capital may be provided by wealthy individual investors, or professionally managed investment funds. Whereas banks tend to focus on a companies' past performance when evaluating them for loans, venture capital firms tend to focus instead on their future potential. As a result, venture capital organizations will examine the features of a business's product, the size of its markets, and its projected earnings.

From 1946 until today, the venture capital firms were dominate in the Private Equity Industry, however, they only work with the upper third of the Private Equity Industry, leaving roughly two third of start-ups to fend for themselves, until now. The Private Equity Industry has been around since the 1890s, only in 2012 has the law been change to allow ordinary people to invest in the embryonic stage of a new business idea in the form of donations and grants. The crowd funding donation and the business formation grant is used by new investors as the first step to entering the lucrative Private Investment Industry.

J.P. Morgan and Leman Brother lasted for more than 100 years, even though Leman Brothers went out of business during the last financial crisis. J.P. Morgan is still around. Today, there are plenty other large financial brokerage firms around such as Merrill Lynch and Price Waterhouse.

Financial Service Brokerage

The concept and term "Prime Brokerage" is generally attributed to the U.S. broker-dealer Furman Selz in the late 1970s. Today we call these brokerages "Financial Service Brokerage" In the pre-prime brokerage marketplace, portfolio management was a significant challenge; money managers had to keep track of all of their own trades, consolidate their positions and calculate their performance, regardless of which brokerage firms executed those trades or maintained those positions. The concept was immediately seen to be successful, and was quickly copied by the dominant bulge bracket brokerage firms such as Morgan Stanley, Bear Stearns, Merrill Lynch, Lehman Brothers, and Goldman Sachs. At this nascent stage, hedge funds were much smaller than they are today and were mostly domestic (U.S.) long-short equities funds. The first overseas prime brokerage business was created by Merrill Lynch International Bank in London in the late 1980s.

Financial Service Brokerage is the generic name for a bundled package of services offered by investment banks to hedge funds. The business advantage to a hedge fund of using a Financial Service Broker is that the Broker provides a centralized securities clearing facility for the hedge fund, and the hedge fund's collateral requirements are netted across all deals handled by the Financial Service Broker. The Broker benefits by earning fees on financing the client's long and short cash and security positions, and by charging, in some cases, fees for clearing other services.

Through the 1980s and 1990s, Financial Service Brokerage was largely an equities-based product, although various prime brokers did supplement their core equities capabilities with basic bond clearing and custody. In addition, prime brokers supplemented their operational function by providing portfolio reporting; initially by messenger, then by fax and today over the web. Over the years, prime brokers have expanded their product and service offerings to include some or all of the full range of fixed income and derivative products, as well as foreign exchange and futures products.

Prime Brokers facilitate hedge fund leverage, primarily through loans secured by the long positions of their clients. In this regard, the Prime Broker is exposed to the risk of loss in the event that the value of collateral held as security declines below the loan value, and the client is unable to repay the deficit. In practice, such conditions arise only in the case of extraordinary volatility or unexpected correlation reversions and are exceedingly rare. Other forms of risk inherent in a prime brokerage include operational risks to reputation.

Equity Capital Funding

The Equity Capital Funding Industry is a broadly used capital investment exchange with private equity investment groups such as; Hedge Funds that are owned by wealthy individuals at one end, and Angel Investors, who invest their own money in start-up business ventures at the other. The average person is familiar with the Public Stock Exchange; they have either invested in stock themselves or have retirement, pension funds and/or IRA's that are invested in the stock market. However, very few are familiar with equity funds which takes a direct stake in a business venture, either in the start-up or growth phase.

The Private Stake Exchanges is made up of private investors ranging from Angel investors to hedge fund owners and managers:

The main difference between the Public Stock Exchange and Private Stake Exchange investors invest in start-ups and expanding small business ventures. While the Public Exchange concentrates on companies that have reached a certain maturity. Today, these two exchanges are playing a key role in investment. The Equity Stake Exchange will bring investing to the masses in the form of early stage business ventures.

Over the next 10 years or so, equity capital funds will engage the masses in the form of entrepreneurship. Every family has at least one entrepreneur; therefore if they are educated properly they can empower their entire community. During the interim period, new entrepreneurs and existing business owners will need business leadership retraining education, new empowerment books, start-up training manuals, games, management and marketing products, goods and services will be needed, as the masses make adjustments to accommodate two different stock exchanges.

In the future equity capital will be the source of real wealth for ordinary people because in the future there will be two major stock exchanges, one private and the other public. Minorities and others, who have been traditionally shut out of the public stock market, will be able to participate in equity funding of start-ups. Equity capital firms could serve as the backbone for the new private stock offerings. The Dow Jones was until recently a family held company and owner of the New York Stock Exchange.

Investment banks
Investment banks help companies and governments and their agencies to raise money by issuing and selling securities in the primary market. They assist public and private corporations in raising funds in the capital markets (both equity and debt), as well as in providing strategic advisory services for mergers, acquisitions and other types of financial transactions.

In the strictest definition, investment banking is the raising of funds, both in debt and equity, and the division handling this is an investment bank, often it is called the "Investment Banking Division" (IBD). However, only a few small firms solely provide this service. Almost all investment banks are heavily involved in providing additional financial services for clients, such as the trading of fixed income, foreign exchange, commodity, and equity securities.

It is therefore acceptable to refer to both the "Investment Banking Division" and other 'front office' divisions such as "Fixed Income" as part of "investment banking," and any employee involved in either side as an "investment banker." Furthermore, one who engages in these activities in-house at a non-investment bank is also considered an investment banker. Many if not most IBD employees consider the title of Investment Banker reserved to them alone and bristle at self-referential use of this title by employees of other IB divisions, especially those engaged in other sales and trading activities.

Investment banks also act as intermediaries in trading for clients. Investment banks differ from commercial banks, which take deposits and make commercial and retail loans. In recent years, however, the lines between the two types of structures have blurred, especially as commercial banks have offered more investment banking services.

In the U.S., the Glass-Steagall Act, initially created in the wake of the Stock Market Crash of 1929, prohibited banks from both accepting deposits and underwriting securities; Glass-Steagall was repealed by the Gramm-Leach-Bliley Act in 1999. Investment banks may also differ from brokerages, which in general assist in the purchase and sale of stocks, bonds, and mutual funds. However some firms operate as both brokerages and investment banks; this includes some of the best known financial service firms in the world.

More commonly used today to characterize what was traditionally termed as "investment banking" is "sell side." This is trading securities for cash or securities (i.e., facilitating transactions, market-making), or the promotion of securities (i.e. underwriting, research, etc.). The "buy side" constitutes the pension funds, mutual funds, hedge funds, and the investing public that consumes the products and services of the sell-side in order to maximize their return on investment. Many firms both buy and sell side components. As with most other endeavors, financial rewards await those who through luck or skill identify opportunity, regardless of whether they are selling or buying.

Private Equity Funds

When a fund buys a majority stake in a company it can restructure its capital, management and organizational structure. Usually target companies are unlisted and held privately and will be restructured over a period of 3-7 years, and then again listed through an IPO. Restructuring may be done through leveraged buyouts, venture capital, growth capital, Angel investing, mezzanine debts, management share participation, programmers and others.

Hedge Fund
As hedge funds have proliferated globally through the 1990s and the current decade, Financial Service Brokerage has become an increasingly competitive field and an important contributor to the overall profitability of the investment banking business. As of 2006, the most successful investment banks reported over two billion dollars each in annual revenue directly attributed to their Financial Service Brokerage operations (source: 2006 annual reports of Morgan Stanley and Goldman Sachs). A Hedge Fund is a

private investment fund charging a performance fee and typically opens to only a limited range of investors. For example, in America, hedge funds are open to accredited investors only. Because of this restriction they are usually exempt from any direct regulation by the SEC, NASD or other regulatory bodies, and the term is used to distinguish them from regulated retail investment funds such as mutual funds, pension funds, and insurance companies.

Hedge Fund activities are limited only by the terms of the contracts governing the particular fund. Hedge Funds can follow complex investment strategies, such as being long or short assets and entering STR into futures, swaps and other derivative contracts. These funds are often organized as limited partnerships in America, and typically invest on behalf of high-net-worth individuals and institutions. A common objective is to generate returns that are not closely correlated to those of the broader financial markets.

Mutual Fund

The definition of a mutual fund is a form of collective investment that pools money from many investors and invests their money in stocks, bonds, dividends, short-term money market instruments, and/or other securities. In a mutual fund, the fund manager trades the fund's underlying securities, realizing capital gains or losses, and collects the dividend or interest income. The investment proceeds are then passed along to the individual investors.

The value of a share of the mutual fund, known as the net asset value per share, is calculated daily based on the total value of the fund divided by the number of shares currently issued and outstanding. Legally known as an "open-end company" under the Investment Company Act of 1940 (the primary regulatory statute governing investment companies), a mutual fund is one of three basic types of investment companies available in the United States.

Outside of the United States (with the exception of Canada, which follows the U.S. model), mutual fund is a generic term for various types of collective investment vehicle.

Pension Fund

A pension is a steady income given to a person (usually after retirement). Pensions are typically payments made in the form of a guaranteed annuity to a retired or disabled employee. Some retirement plans accumulate a cash balance that a retiree can draw upon at retirement, rather than promising annuity payments. These are often also called pensions. In either case, a pension created by an employer for the benefit of an employee is commonly referred to as an occupational or employer pension. Labor unions, the government, or other organizations may also fund pensions. Occupational pensions are a form of deferred compensation, usually advantageous to employee and employers for tax reasons. Many pensions also contain an insurance aspect, since they often will pay benefits to survivors or disabled beneficiaries, while annuity income insures against the risk of longevity. While other vehicles (certain lottery payouts, for example, or an annuity) may provide a similar stream of payments, the common use of the term pension is to describe the payments a person receives upon retirement, usually under pre-determined legal and/or contractual terms.

V.   Business Model Plans

In the era of the Billion Dollar Startup the Business Model Plan is an essential document for entrepreneurs and existing business owners that are seeking equity and venture capital.

The Business Model Plan is a detailed document that maybe used by both business owners and investors that are new to private equity investing. It includes a content outline page that simplifies the business planning process by making it easy to read. It uses full-page numbers and sub-topic page numbers to make it easy to locate key parts of the plan without reading all sections. When this document is presented to investors it provides a road map for growth that can be shared with financial institutions and others. The Business Model Plan also help evaluates the capability of the management team, as well as the future growth potential of the business enterprise you want to invest in.

The Business Model Plan provides the information necessary to help small investors compete with angel investors, venture capitalists and others for quality business ventures to invest in. Since, the 1930's non-accredited investors were not allowed to invest in early stage start-ups, as such; there was no Private Sector Business Infrastructure that could assist those that wanted to invest in Small & Medium Enterprises (SMEs). They are the largest business classification in the world, accounting for more than 70% of all new jobs created. In this highly competitive business environment individual investors and business owners need a document that is prepared exclusively for them.

The Business Model Plan is a document that can be used by anyone seeking equity and venture capital. Moreover, it can be used as an analysis tool by accredited and non-accredited investors. It's an excellent document to evaluate business projects with no previous track record of earnings. This document can be used in all industries where equity or venture capital is needed. The Business Model Plan can never be outgrown because of the professional development and support staff attached to each software writing platform used by business owners before and after funding.

The Business Model Plan is also used as an investment tool to assist Early Stage Investor with determining the Proof of Concept for business venture before they invest in them. It's an excellent document to evaluate business projects with no previous track record of earnings. This document can be used in all industries where equity or venture capital is needed. The Business Model Plan can never be outgrown because of the professional development and support staff attach to the software writing platform that can provide assistance to business owners before and after funding. The Network connects existing business owners to new sources of investment capital, using virtual business and marketing institutions included in the Equity Capital Access Network.

The Equity Capital Access Network connects existing business owners to new sources of investment capital, using virtual business and marketing institutions, they will need before and after funding. The Business Model Plan provides the information necessary to help small investors compete with angel investors, venture capitalists and others for quality business ventures to invest in.

Types of Business Model Plans

The Business Model Plan is the first step for entrepreneurs and business owners to prepare their ventures for equity funding requirements. This step lets the business owner assemble information starting with the basic business and marketing planning process. This stage of the business model building process may be skipped by a client that has already completed a business and marketing plan before enrollment. There is business development modules that allow all information gathered to fit neatly into the finished business model plan. Once printed these plans will help in the second stage of the business model development process where outside help may be required.

The rapid rise of the billion dollar startup has cause price of early stage business ventures to skyrocket. Therefore, in this era the Business Model Plan is an essential document for entrepreneurs and existing business owners that are seeking equity and venture capital.

General Business Model Plan
General Business Model Plan combines the information assembled from the business and marketing plans. The Incubator is compartmentalized by separate modules, given entrepreneur's different styles to choose from. Once a choice is made, the entrepreneur will fill in the required information including the income projection and balance sheet and then a version of the business model plan may be printed. However, the content is limited to information found in the business and marketing plan section. These plans can be printed or sent electronically, this plan's information can also be transferred to the endorsement business model plan module.

Once all the information has been placed in the proper modules a printed version may be obtained. In this business module the entrepreneurs can get additional help as they need it from qualified professionals listed in this section. You can assemble an entire team before you begin the building process, or you can hire them as needed. Each professional listed for this section has special skill-sets needed in the writing of a Business Model Plan.

Endorsed Business Model Plan

The traditional business and marketing plan were written primarily by entrepreneurs seeking debts financing. It's still required by banks and other lending institutions that make loans. Small business owners and new entrepreneurs seeking equity funding for an existing business are encouraged to submit a more detail document called a Business Model Plan. Once written properly this plan can help make the venture being presented better understood. The business and marketing plans are not discarded it's merely combined to make-up the business model plan.

The Endorsed Business Model Plan serves as a guide to a business projects for the activity of the business venture in a stated period of time. In order to keep the information current it must be updated frequently. In addition to the information you will find in the business and marketing plans, this model requires that you complete a target market research analysis, feasibility study, and a three to five year income projection. If this business model plan is going to be submitted for the certification of a business model a balance sheet and investor's forecast must be added.

An Endorsement Business Model Plan Package allows subscribers to select and assemble their own Business Development Team, from a list of pre-qualified professionals. The major advantage of a team focused plan is the attachment of business developers and consultants that can provide support to business owners before and after funding.

Certified Business Model Plan

The Certified Business Model Plan is a viable option when seeking equity capital from a new class of investors that will consider your business model exclusively. A Certified Business Model Plan starts out with the highest Investment Score. The weakness & strength of the business model plan will have a direct impact on the initial investment points assigned. This model building strategy requires that the owner, conduct, in-depth market analysis, feasibility and target market research studies about their products and services.

Once, printed these plans will help in the second stage of the business model development process where outside help maybe required. This 1st stage of the business model building process may be skipped by clients that have already completed business and marketing plans before enrollment. Business owners with Certified Business Models will receive a venture capital access score that allow them to contact investors directly. Business Model Plan Software can generate Custom Business Model Plans that can be presented to financial institutions and private investors.

Software Writing Platform

The Business Model Plan Writing Software use Independent & Major Service Providers to assist business owners that need help in writing their business model plans. Additionally, Independent & Major Service Providers are available to provide additional assistance and support when needed. BusinessModelPlans.Com has a Software Writing Platform for subscribers and others that are seeking equity or venture capital. The Business Model Plan Software will be offered by subscription to new entrepreneurs and existing business owners. Business Model Plan Writers have a strong background in business plan writing and/or business consulting services to small business owners.

Model Plan Writers and Consultants

The Business Model Plan Software Writing Platform provides support assistance to new entrepreneurs and existing business owners, using professionals and practical consultants. The major advantage of a team focused business development process is the attachment of business developers that can provide support for business and franchise model owners before and after funding. Business Model Plan writers and consultants are assigned to subscribers that need help in compiling and writing a Business Model Plan. A well written Business Model Plan aids in the assembling of information to build a business model that can be certified. Likewise, it will aid in the developing of a franchise agreement. With annual updates, the Business Model Plan can be used for the life of your business, even when you develop a franchise business system.

Business Model Plans are used by both private investors and business owners. Independent Business Developer (IBD) is the team leader that oversees the business writing process from beginning to certification. Qualified candidates must have a strong background in business writing and/or business consulting. There are two types of Business Developers, the independent business developer outside the business incubators and/or franchise incubator accelerators.

Independent Business Developers are project leaders that work directly with owners who are developing business models and/or franchises. They help business owners gather and prioritize their business information including: research information, and marketing strategy. Business developers are also involved in the recruiting and training of professional and practical consultants that are members of the business development team.

These developers work in the pre-business writing and certification division. They both work with business owners that are seeking equity and venture capital or preparing their business venture for development or conversion into a franchise. Individuals selected must have a strong background in providing assistance to entrepreneurs. Once, selected they are attached to business development incubators where they provide assistance in development and certifying business models and franchises. These professionals may also be eligible to join our Business Development Teams and provide Business Model Plan writing assistance to subscribers in their area.

The Virtual Business Incubator System contains a Growth & Development Platform for small business owners who want to grow and expand their business ventures beyond their local markets. Business owners who subscriber can use other member programs and services to enhance their growth. For example: if your business need direct mail, you may be able to incorporate a private label service into your business with all back room services handled by affiliate partners.

Single Software Subscriber User

Business opportunities offered include; Dot-Com Business Incubator, Franchises, Business Model Plan Software User License Agreement and the Business Model Plan Software Marketing Agency. Attorneys and others that provide assistance to new entrepreneurs and existing business owners may also be eligible to join our business development teams and provide Business Model Plan writing assistance to subscribers in their area. There is an independent distributorship that maybe added for the software, before it becomes part of the Franchise Business System; which will limit outside user rights.

Professionals & Group User License

The Business Model Plan Software is offered to both single and group users including professionals such as: accountants, attorneys' tax preparers, bookkeepers, grant writers and others that currently provide assistance to entrepreneurs. Enrolled professionals may also be eligible to join our business development teams and provide Business Model Plan writing assistance to subscribers in their area.

The Dot-Com Business Incubator offer comprehensive development services for Certified Business Models and Franchises. These Certified Business Model & Franchises are built on Growth and Development Platforms where a business development team is assigned to each project that is being certified. Certification is provided by 3rd party verifying organizations that can test the core concept and business structure in the actual marketplace. The team effort shares in the business concept and management knowledge from the beginning until the enterprise is funded; team members make themselves available to business owners when needed.

The Dot-Com Business Incubator is accessible to anyone with a computer and internet access. Business developers and other support associates are attached to incubators to assist business owners and subscribers who use our Business Model Plan writing services. There are two Virtual Business Incubators with a Business Model Plan Software Writing Platform attached to them. (Dot-Com Business Incubator and the MicroBusiness Development Incubator). The software assistance agreements are leased to individuals and professionals for a stated period of time and for a fee stated in the contract. There are two forms of software assistance agreements offered, one is for general user and the other is an exclusive territory user agreement.

Certified Business Models & Franchises

Certified business models and franchises that are built in Virtual Business Development Incubators are developed and tested in the actual marketplace by 3rd party verifying organizations, such as the National Association of Home Based Businesses (NAHBB) and the Micro-Business Enterprise Association. These two organizations have business developers and consultants attached; they assist business owners before and after funding. The Certified Business Model or Franchise is a more predictable method of growing a business, that's why it's preferred by private investors, banks and other financial institutions.

The Certified Business Model is also used to increase the investment scores needed by new entrepreneurs and existing business owners who are seeking equity capital from a new class of angel investors and venture capitalists. The Investment Scoring System has brought major changes to the venture capital community and brought into existence the Investment Access Provider (IAP) and Equity Capital Manager (ECM) two financial specialists who cater to high net-worth investors. Angel investors and others use these providers to screen their investment opportunities based on a predetermined scoring range.

Business owners, who select to have their business model certified, use a Business Trade Organizations such as the National Association of Home Based Businesses and Micro Business Enterprise Association. The Network offers pre-investment assistance to new clients that need growth capital coverage because the Equity Capital Access Network accepts start-up business ventures for funding long before they are ready for an Initial Public Offering (IPO).

The first stage in the development of the Certified Business Model and the Franchise Model is the creation of a Business Model Plan. This management tool helps to define the future goals and objectives of a company for potential lenders and investors. Business owners who use the Dot-Com Business Incubator – Business Model Plan Software can produce a document that's used to apply for funding from private investors and financial institutions. Moreover, a Business Model Plan will help a business owner communicate their company's management and marketing strategy to others including the management staff.

The Business Model Plan is a first step guide for entrepreneurs and business owners, to prepare their ventures for equity funding. This step allows the business owner to assemble information starting with basic business and marketing data. There is business formation modules that allow all information gathered to fit neatly into the finished Business Model Plan.

The major advantage of a team focused business development process is the attachment of business developers that can provide support for business and franchise model owners before and after funding. The business model development teams include lawyers, accountants, business teachers, consultants, business developers, marketing & management professionals, financial counselors and others. These professionals provide the support needed when entrepreneurs need additional assistance for such things as their business plans and writing of income forecasts.

Certified Business Model
A Certified Business Model is a completed version of an Endorsed Business Model. The electronic version of this model is a continuation of the Endorsed Business Model Plan, with the addition of a space for the third party organization evaluation team comments. For example: the business owner's version of his management team experience may be 60 years, but documents show that they have only 50. Both versions will be included in the model plan, however, the third party verifying organization figure will be added to the comment sections. Likewise, an asking price for a product may be higher than the price point of their nearest competitor; it too will appear in the evaluation team comment section. Recommendations will also be included in the evaluation teams comment section of the plan.

The Certified Business Model is a predictable method for growing a business that's why it's preferred by new millennium venture capitalists, private investors, banks and other financial institutions. The Certified Business Model will become an even more viable option, when selected equity capital access sources identify a new class of investors that will consider these models exclusively.

A Certified Business Model Plan starts out with the highest Investment Score. The weakness & strength of the business model plan will have a direct Impact on the initial investment points assigned. This model building strategy requires that the owner conduct in-depth market analysis, feasibility and target market research studies about their products and services.

A well written Business Model Plan aids in the assembling of information to build a business model that can be certified. It will aid you while you're developing your franchise agreement. The plan has whole page numbers and sub-page numbers, making it easy for the investors to locate key parts of the plan without reading unwanted sections. This new business planning tool enables new entrepreneurs to know the business venture better as opposed other methods.

The Certified Business Model is a viable option when seeking equity capital from a new class of investors that will consider your business model exclusively. A Certified Business Model Plan starts out with the highest Investment Score. The weakness & strength of the business model plan will have a direct impact on the initial investment points assigned. This model building strategy requires that the owner, conduct, in-depth market analysis, feasibility and target market research studies about their products and services.

Pre-Business Planning
There are two types of software packages found in the Dot-Com Business Incubator. The first is a leadership training module that includes a Business Model Plan Template which allows subscribers to assemble information under major and sub-topics. Once

completed, the subscriber can create a printed document that's unique to their business, which can be presented to potential investors, lending institutions and others. These business model plans will help to raise the investment point score, which are required by a new class of investors. The minimum standard for enrollment in the Virtual Incubator Business System is the completion of a Business Model Plan. It is completed by business owners expanding beyond their local markets.

Business Model Plan templates were developed for individuals who placed information into compartmental data modules. Once the data is imputed into the Business Model Plan template, it will produce a print document for which the owner can present to lending institutions and others, including venture capital firms. The first stage in the developing of a business or franchise model is the creation of a Business Model Plan. This plan is a management tool that helps to define a company's goals and objectives for potential lenders and investors. Business owners who use the Dot-Com Business Incubator Business Model Plan template can produce a document that is used to apply for funding from private investors and financial institutions. A Business Model Plan will also help you to communicate your company's management and marketing strategy to others including your management staff.

Equity Capital Access Network is a one-stop shop for private investors seeking early stage start-ups and expanding franchise projects. The Equity Capital Access Network provides development & support platforms for business owners and entrepreneurs, seeking equity and venture capital funding.

ModelFran Marketing Distributors

Business ModelFran™ offer Business Model Plan writing assistance and consulting services through special agreements and independent agency outlets. The Dot-Com Business Incubator ™

offers comprehensive business development services to four types of business and franchise models. They include the General Business Model, Endorsement Business Model and the Certified Business Model. Business owners with Certified Business Models will get a venture capital access scores and will be allowed to contract investors directly, if they choose too.

The Dot-Com Business Incubator™ includes a Business Model Plan Software that can generate a Custom Business Model Plans that can be presented to financial institutions and private investors. To make business model plans and business and franchise model development service available to all, the Dot-Com Business Incubator is accessible to anyone with a computer and internet access. Business developers and other support associates are attached to incubators to assist business owners and subscribers that use the business model plan writing services.

Business and Franchise Models
The highest initial scores are assigned to Certified Business and Franchise models that show great promise. Certified Business and Franchise Models are viable options for a new class of investors who are searching for more structured business ventures to invest in. Once certified by a business or trade organization, the business is assigned a code guide number, that separate them form their competitors. Either a Home Business Identity Classification (HBIC) or Micro-Business Trade Classification (MBTC) is assigned to these business models or franchises. Certified Business Models are assigned private Business Trade Group (BTG) numbers. Only certified business models may carry their own private BTG numbers. These numbers can be used to start your own Infinity Marketing Circle.

The business model development program include many types of support groups such as business development teams, which are made-up of lawyers, accountants, business teachers, consultants, business developers, marketing & management professional, financial counselors and others. These professionals provide the support needed when entrepreneurs need additional assistance for such things as their business plans and writing of income forecasters. Professionals such as; accountants and attorneys that provide assistance to new entrepreneurs and existences to new entrepreneur and exist business owners that are seeking equity and/or venture capital, maybe eligible to join a business development team and provide business model plan writing assistance to subscribers in their areas. Exclusive territory rights are also available.

Business Leadership Training Courses
The Dot-Com Business Incubator System also provides business leadership courses for individuals and entrepreneurs who want to become micro-business teachers, consultant's business developers and franchise marketers. These train-the-trainer courses provide trainee who successfully complete all course requirements with professional credentials that's used to assist business owners who want to build successful Business and Franchise Models. Teachers and consultants who are certified can assist individuals who want a reliable source of angel investors that provide equity capital. Once certified, these professionals can teach and/or provide assistance to business owners and entrepreneurs who want to build a business model plan that can be presented to equity capital investors. This training program allows newly trained students to graduate into a complete network support system.

VI. Franchise Incubator Accelerator

The Franchise Incubator Accelerator offers business model development and equity funding platforms for high growth companies. The Franchise Incubator Accelerator was established as a one-stop shop for business owners who need both business model development and equity funding. The Franchise Incubator Accelerator shorting the time between concept and when a venture reaches the marketplace ready to conduct business. The Franchise Incubator Accelerator was established to provide equity capital funding access to business owners with certified business models or franchises. All accepted projects begin as a Certified Business Model that can be converted into a franchise.

The Franchise Incubator Accelerator allows small business owners' to by-pass banks and other traditional lending institutions and go directly to private investors to raise equity funds. However, there are up front charges for transforming a Certified Business Model into a Franchise. The enrollment fees may include a percentage of the equity shares in the company being developed. The development process for a Virtual Business Model starts during at the embryonic stage. There are two distinct stages, the first is the business formation stage and the second is the franchise development stage in a Virtual Business Incubator.

Virtual Business Incubator System

The Virtual Business Incubator System is a major part of a Business and Franchise Model Development Program. It provides business development services from concept to franchising. The Virtual Business Incubator System includes three types of online Incubators; Dot-Com Business Incubators, Exporters Incubator of America, and MicroBusiness Development Incubators. These Incubators are based on the Internet and therefore can deliver business development services to entrepreneurs with existing enterprises that are capable of growing beyond their local markets. This is a private business development service that provides assistance to entrepreneurs and others who need a comprehensive Business Model Plan to give to potential lending institutions and/or equity capital funding sources.

When the Equity Capital Access System is combined with a Virtual Business Incubator System, these two services are compartmentalized from one another and administrated separately. However, equity capital funding access may not be granted without an approved Certified Business Model or Franchise that is built in a Virtual Business Development Incubator. The Virtual Business Incubator System is a major part of a Business and Franchise Model Development Program that includes Franchise Incubator Accelerator and Private Equity Capital Centers.

It provides business development services from concept to franchising and a private business development service that provides assistance to entrepreneurs and others that need a comprehensive Business Model Plan to provide to potential lending institutions and other equity capital funding sources.

Virtual Business Development Incubators can provide Small & Medium Enterprise (SME) owners with a growth development marketing strategy that can be implemented in stages. The Virtual Business Incubator System contains growth and development platforms for small business owners who want to grow and expand their business ventures beyond their local markets. Business owners who are members of a Virtual Business Network use others members programs and services to enhance their business enterprises.

The Virtual Business Incubator System is a private business development service that provides assistance to entrepreneurs and others who need a comprehensive Business Model Plan and equity capital funding sources. This Business and Franchise Model Development Program provides business development services from concept to franchising.

Model Development Platform

Using successful ownerless business ventures that can be developed into franchises over a period of time is now a national trend in Early Stage Franchising. The old business philosophy presupposes that an individual who started a business venture was best suited to grow it to maturity. This is an outdated philosophy in the 21st Century. Business development teams are attached to a virtual business incubator system. These business teams are trained to build industry driven business models and franchises in business formation and development incubators.

In order to create opportunities for future generations, there must be industry driven models built around successful business enterprises that can be grown into a franchise. Concept Starter began the Business Formation Grant Program because of the difficulties small investors will face when searching for quality business ventures to invest in, once Title III of the Jobs Act is fully implemented. ConceptStarter.Net is a Virtual Business Formation Incubator that uses business formation grants as seed funds to develop a Business Formation Model from the embryonic stage of a new business idea.

Business Formation Incubators are based on the Internet and provides business formation services and access to crowd funding donations, business formation grants, and equity capital funding for selected owners with a business formation model plan. There are two types of concept funding projects accepted by these incubators: the first is capital raised for business formation models, and the second is for existing business with owners that are seeking equity capital to grow.

Business Development Model

Certified business models and franchises are built in Virtual Business Development Incubators and tested in the actual marketplace by 3rd party verifying organizations that include the National Association of Home Based Businesses (NAHBB) and the Micro-Business Enterprise Association (MBEA) and now the Early Stage Franchise Association (ESFA). These three associations have business developers and consultants attached that can assist business owners before and after funding

Dot-Com Business Incubator

Dot-Com Business Incubators offers pre-planning assistance and comprehensive business model development services for certified business models and franchises. These certified business and franchise models are built on growth and development platforms where a business development team is assigned to each project that is being certified. The Dot-Com Business Incubator is the first stop for individuals seeking funding to finance their business ventures.

The Dot-Com Business Incubator also provides pre-planning assistance for business owners that need industry and market research. This incubator system can also connect you to outside development agencies that can offer additional support and development services to new owners with existing business ventures.

The Dot-Com Business Incubator is a Virtual Business Development System that uses the Internet to provide fast track pre-business planning assistance and advance business model development services for new entrepreneurs and existing business owners. This online service connects local development agencies to service centers which provide support and development services to new and existing business ventures. Once implemented, these incubators can provide face-to-face contacts with clients that need business development team assistance.

The major advantage of a team focused business development process is that a business developer can provide additional support for the business and franchise model they develop before and after funding. Team members make themselves available to business owners when needed. This allows team members to share in the business concept and management knowledge from the beginning until the enterprise is funded.

The Dot-Com Business Incubator offers comprehensive development services for certified business models and franchises that are built on growth and development platforms. Dot-Com Business Incubator specializes in business models and franchises. This is Virtual Business Development Incubator that specializes in start-ups and expanding business ventures that are seeking equity capital from angel investors and venture capitalists. A Dot-Com Business Incubator offers new entrepreneurs and existing business owners who want to apply for venture capital for funding a unique document to increase their chances to raise the capital they need.

The Dot-Com Business Incubator offers comprehensive development assistance for business and franchise models. The Dot-Com Business Incubator provides services that include the Business Model Plan template. They include the General Business Model, Endorsement Business Model, and the Certified Business Model. Business owners with certified business models will get venture capital access scores that will allow them to contract investors directly.

The Dot-Com Business Incubator is a virtual business development service for business owners and entrepreneurs who need a Business Model Plan. Business model plans are preferred by private investors and new millennium venture capitalists; because they provide in-depth information for investors that need to evaluate the investment opportunity before funding is offered. These plans contain equity capital access information from pre-business planning to advance business development.

The Dot-Com Business Incubator generates custom business model plan templates that can be presented to financial institutions and private investors. Business owners and new entrepreneurs start the process by subscribing to an on-line business model plan writing service. The Dot-Com Business Incubator offers business model plan assistance. The Dot-Com Business Incubator is home to the Business Model Plan used by venture capitalists to evaluate investment opportunities before they invest. The Business Model Plan Template has compartment modules that correspond with major topics and sub-topics you select for your plan.

The template can produce the following types of Business Model Plans: 1) The General Business Model Pan, can be used by an individual with moderate computer skills. 2) The Endorsement Business Model Plan allows the subscriber to select and assemble their own teams, from a list of pre-qualified professionals or they can use them as needed. Once completed, a finished document can be printed with your business name and logo on the front cover. If you become a long time subscriber you can make regular updates to your plan as your business grows or you can build another business model plan with or without assistance from a business development team or other service providers.

The Dot-Com Business Incubator includes a Business Model Plan template that can generate custom business model plans that can be presented to financial institutions and private investors. The Dot-Com Business Incubator is accessible to anyone with a computer and internet access. Business developers and other support associates are attached to incubators to assist business owners and new entrepreneurs who need their services.

The Dot-Com Business Incubator™ includes a Business Model Plan Software that can generate Custom Business Model Plans that can be presented to financial institutions and private investors. To make business that our business model plans services are available to all, the Dot-Com Business Incubator is accessible to anyone with a computer and internet access. Business developers and other support associates are attached to incubators to assist business owners and subscribers who need their services.

Investors like certified business modes because they provide a more predictable method of growing a business. Anyone applying for secondary and third level of participation will have the support of two business trade organizations, including the National Association of Home Based Businesses (NAHBB) and the Micro Business Enterprise Association (MBEA), both have third level verifying teams certified business models and franchises. The business model core concept and business structure is tested in the actual marketplace.

MicroBusiness Development Incubators
The Small Business Network has authorized the establishment of MicroBusiness Development Incubators. These public and private franchise models will fill a major gap left by federal and states economic development strategies. They provide the transformation process necessary in the virtualization of a business model. Major Service Providers and others with special skills may be invited to serve in on a Business Development Team.

MicroBusiness Development Incubators service small and home based businesses that specialize in more than 300 Business Trade Groups. MicroBusiness development incubators vary in the way they deliver services to the clients they serve. Successful completion of a business incubation program increases the likelihood that a company will stay in business for the long term: Historically, a large percentage of incubator graduates stay in business. Incubators are separate from research and technology because they are dedicated to start-ups and early-stage business ventures.

The old philosophy of starting a business by trial and error has given way to concept formation services that include access to equity capital. The new field of Business Concept Formation will provide a more predictable way to grow a small business venture from an embryonic or idea stage, thereby creating a more manageable business system for fast growth.

Certified Franchise Marketer (CFM)

The Business & Franchise Model Development Program includes a comprehensive franchise marketing system. It has business development teams attached to provide business owners with assistance when needed. The Certified Franchise Marketer's training course is taught by both correspondence and on-line in the Dot-Com Business Incubator using business leadership training software. A Certified Franchise Marketer (CFM) is the chief sales and marketing representative for the Franchise Opportunity Network. Once certified, they can teach seminars, workshops and consult business owners that want to expand their businesses beyond local markets. They market and sell certified business models and franchises in assigned territories. CFMs have the exclusive marketing rights to all business models and franchises in the network.

There are other business development services in the marketplace run by business consultants that provide preplanning business assistance and model development services. Moreover, they can build distribution networks and outlets for business models and franchises.

Independent Consultant Firms

Venture capitalist firms provide a traditional service for private business owners who want to take their company public. There are major differences between a venture capitalist firm and Equity Source Company with Angel Investors. Since the dot-com era, venture capitalists have been inundated with funding requests. However, many only want to invest in high-tech companies they can eventually take public, rejecting more than 90% of all other funding proposals without giving the business owners any feedback about why they were turned down for funding.

Many of today's equity source companies use some type of Investment Scoring System, which gives the owner that apply to them for venture funding a measurable means to determine the strength and weakness of their investment opportunity.

Business Development Team

The Network offers pre-investment assistance to new clients that need growth capital coverage, because the Equity Capital Access Network accepts start-up business ventures for funding long before they are ready for an Initial Public Offering (IPO). Our Franchise Incubator Accelerator helps small business owners' by-pass banks and other traditional lending institutions, thereby allowing them to go directly to investors.

The Dot-Com Business Development Team members can also assist clients with team selection, if they subscribe to this level of service. The 3rd level program is the certifying of business models and franchises. Certification is provided by 3rd party verifying organizations that test the core concept and business structure in the actual marketplace. Business owners, who select to have their business model certified, use a Business Trade Organization such as the National Association of Home Based Businesses or Micro Business Enterprise Association.

In the 21st Century, the technology revolution in communications, including the Internet satellites and other communications devices, make it easy to view a new business model in its inception; therefore making it impossible to use the cookie cutter model of franchising made possible by McDonald's, which has grown to symbolize the franchise. In the fast moving global marketplace, a business must start off with an eye towards franchising. Therefore, a new entrepreneur must build a business model from the first day it starts that will alternatively lead to a franchise.

A successful business model must contain a marketing strategy that includes a business development team that is always available for consulting, because a successful business in today's marketplace must be ready and capable of constant changes. The Certified Business Model is the only business structure that allows a business owner to test the method of growth before it is converted into a franchise business system.

A business model and franchise goes hand-in-hand, which allows a business to be duplicated much faster than the old franchise model. The Certified Business Model is the preferred method of growth by new millennium venture capitalists. One of the requirements of a venture capitalist for a new entrepreneur before they grant funding was learned through the dot-com boom era-owners. It is necessary to have the capability to recruit a strong business management team, without resources it was hard to assemble. However, today the Certified Business Model comes with a pool of independent businesses and support associates for hire on an as-needed basis. When a business owner applies for venture funding, one of the first things the venture capitalists looks for is a compliant business development team.

Independent Business Developers

Small business consultants, accountants and others with experience in assisting small businesses may become certified business developers. Business developers are attached to development incubators, where they can assist in the building and certifying of business models and franchises. Qualified candidates must undergo training in a home correspondence course. After the satisfactory completion of the training program, the National Association of Home Based Home based Businesses and the Micro-Business Enterprise Association MBEA will designate them as a Certified Business Developer (CBD). With time and more experience, a CBD can rise to the rank of Master Business Developer (MBD). This is the very top the rank in the fields of business development and consulting.

Business Development Services

The new global marketplace demands a more intelligent approach to building a business such as; feasibility studies and target market analysis of the industry you want to enter, this is an essential part of the selection and growth process. To meet this demand, the Equity Capital Access Network authorized Dot-Com Business Incubators, which includes small business development modules for business owners and new entrepreneurs, assembling information for their business model plans. Attached to this on-line model building system are train-the-trainer courses for micro-business teachers, consultants and counselors. Each enrollee can work at their own pace, when they complete all requirements; the system will award them a certificate.

Once certified, these professionals can teach and assist existing business owners and entrepreneurs in assembling information necessary to build a business model that equity capital investors will want to fund. This new training program will bring new teachers and consultants to the Equity Capital Access Network. These new independent trainers and marketing consultants will have a vested interest in the success of the network.

The Independent marketing representatives assist small business owners and others that are seeking equity financing sources for their particular business ventures. They're paid a commission on the gross amount awarded to the business owner from an investor. Entrepreneurs who want to be a Venture Capital Counselor can operate an agency or brokerage service from home.

NAHBB Franchise Development Group
The NAHBB Franchise Development Group is in charge of the new business planning and model development service on the Equity Capital Access Network. These services are offered through the Dot-Com Business Incubator for start-ups and expansion business ventures, seeking funding from Angel Investors and New Millennium Venture Capitalists. To make these capital sources a viable option, a new class of investors was identified that accepts certified business models and franchises exclusively. The business model building process includes the wide use of the Investment Scoring System that informs entrepreneurs about what Angel Investors want. This allows business owners and participating entrepreneurs to opt out of an "unaided" program and apply directly to a private network that provides full service.

For those who need venture capital to start and grow a business, ECANN.NET is the main connecting website for start-ups and existing businesses seeking equity capital from private investors. ECANN.NET is the on-line infrastructure and the main connecting website to business planning and development services necessary to prepare a business for the new Investment Scoring System that is now used by a new class of investors. Angel investors and investment access companies use the Investment Score as a analysis tool to determine the viability of a business enterprise as it relates to future value. Investors use ECANN.NET to find certified business models and franchise investment opportunities early while they start and expand.

FastTrack Business Development

The Fast Track Business Model Development Programs include business development teams with a pool of independent business and support associates from which to choose. The FastTrack Business Development Program converts successful business models into franchises in months, instead of years. Unlike the old cookie cutter franchise model made famous by McDonald and Burger King fast food outlets. It took years to build their original models. The highest level professional on Wall Street is the Investment Banker and in the start-up sector of the economy, the top professional is a Certified Business Developer. Together they form the skill-set needed to provide comprehensive development services necessary for a business venture that is started today, to someday become a public trade company.

A Business Development Team consists of marketing consultants, management consultants, lawyers, accountants, business developers, and many others public and private professionals. These business development teams are attached to Small Business Development Incubators and other affiliate entrepreneurial training systems.

Buying a franchise falls somewhere in the middle of working with someone else and starting a business of your own. The main difference is that you are not starting from scratch; you already have a recognized product or service. In addition to name recognition, you will have a proven business plan, operation and training manual. There are many definitions of what constitutes a franchise including those found in state statutes.

The most convenient analysis and definitions come from the Federal Trade Commission (FTC), a government agency that has nationwide regulatory power in this field. The FTC recognizes two types of business relationships that qualify for regulation. One is a business opportunity and the other is a distributorship model. To build national and international business models and franchises, there has to be modern day institutions devoted exclusively to business development, support, marketing, management and financing new start-ups and high growth potential companies.

There are three distinct incubators in the small business development incubator system. The Virtual Business Development Incubator offers services that include the certification of business and franchise models, and the Exporters Incubator of America, the oldest of the three, offers certification to independent exporters and importers, and Export/Import Management Companies that uses our International Traders Network. The Franchise Incubator Accelerator builds both single and dual unit franchise systems.

Franchise Business System

Traditional, franchise market expansion was based entirely on the duplication of single-unit franchises. The term cookie cutter franchise model was originated to describe this method of growth. The single unit franchise represents the original franchise model where a specific business was created and depended on duplicating every function exactly, for the life of the venture. It was then duplicated over and over again with both the franchisor and franchisee taking their percentages of the profits. This marketing strategy provides private investors and others owners with the opportunity to buy both franchises, before they are split and sold separately.

There are two distinct methods of establishing a franchise system; single and dual-unit franchising. Although, single and multi-unit franchising offers two different methods of franchising, they both have proven to be successful. The addition of dual-unit franchising has proven to be even more efficient and profitable than its predecessors.

The Dual Unit Franchise System works well because it allows the developer to gather facts on where the inefficiencies lie within an industry, where profitable opportunities lie, and whether or not it is beneficial to select a particular type of venture in the first place.

The old franchise model success was based on the principle that their models could not be changed. Today's franchise models have the ability to adapt to the changing speed of technology, including the internet. Franchise models built in this manner are usually built in a small business development incubator using a business development team.

Industry Driven Model

An industry driven venture encompasses an entire industry. They are built around a selected industry's product or service with a website and other support needed for the business model selected. The Industry Driven Model can use a marketing strategy that includes single, dual, and multi-unit franchises.

Industry Driven Models are built on growth and development platforms which allow them to be changed constantly and be updated. Because of the speed of the new global marketplace, trying to find a successful business model in which to grow a modern franchise is nearly impossible. The old cookie cutter franchise was ideal at the time however, because of the size of the global marketplace with all of its complexities; an Industry Driven

Model is now the best choice. Well known Industry Driven Models include; Google, Facebook and Amazon, to name a few.

Industry driven models uses strategies that include marketing platforms for expansion and growth in fast growing industries. These early stage franchise models are built in a business development incubator by a team of experienced business developers and consultants.

Today, large companies are using technology and the Internet to monopolize traditional industries. This trend was started by Mega Stores such as; Wal-Mart and Target Department Stores. These large retail outlets have destroyed small neighborhood businesses and their suppliers. Industry driven models does the opposite, they invite successful business owners from selected industries to participate and in many cases build their business models around a successful local business with which consumers are familiar. This allows owners to become a part of the business foundation, if they meet the participation requirements.

There is a new class of professional consultants that provide business formation service to early stage start-ups. They have the necessary skills to assist business owners and new entrepreneurs in the building of business formation and model development services. These professional and practical consultants must are capable of evaluating new business ideas from the embryonic stage to a franchise business system.

In the fast paced global marketplace certified business models & franchises are the new starting point for entrepreneurs who want to own their own business ventures. The world's markets are too large to open a single franchise one at a time. The only alternative left to business owners who want to achieve national & international market saturation in their lifetimes is through multi-unit franchising.

Franchise Stock Exchange

The Franchise Stock Exchange (FSE) provides equity and venture capital platforms for certified business models and franchise business systems. The Franchise Stock Exchange is a venture capital formation service for business owners with certified business models and franchises.

This Investment Capital Access Network is where business owners with franchise business systems come to secure equity funds to grow their business ventures. The Franchise Stock Exchange was established for owners with new and existing franchise systems that need equity and venture capital for fast growth. This private Franchise Stock Exchange specializes in certified business models and franchises. The FSE also assists prequalified investors that want to purchase the exclusive rights to new and existing franchise systems with franchise territories for multi-unit franchise outlets. The FSE offers franchise business systems, territory lease/sell agreements, plus exclusive rights to developed and undeveloped franchise territories.

Business Capital Platform

In the post Internet boom-era, developing a business model around your concept is the best way for a start-up business to obtain venture capital funding. Entrepreneurs seeking venture funding with third party verified business models and successful performance records, stands a better chance of attracting venture capital. The investment community now gives a business venture less than three years to show a profit. Therefore, a successful business model or franchise must be built on a growth and development platform where it can receive additional assistance when needed, and where help is always at their fingertips.

Certified business models and franchises that are built in Small Business Development Incubators are done so, at the request of concept owners and/or investors. This business development program builds business models and franchises for owners who need a special class of model used exclusively for equity funding. These business models are the key to new global marketing strategy.

In today's fast pace global marketplace, new business ventures need a predictable business structure that starts with a Business Model Plan. The Franchise Incubator Accelerator allows business owners to write a Business Model Plan for their business systems in the Dot-Com Business Incubator, seek financing on the Franchise Stock Exchange, and showcase certified business models and franchises on Electronic Wall Street.

The Modern American Entrepreneurship Philosophy encourages the evolution of business ventures on growth and development platforms with business development teams available to owners when needed. A business development team consists of marketing consultants, management consultants, lawyers, accountants and certified international traders. These business development teams are attached to small business development incubators.

The endorsement of certified business models and franchises are valuable because these two business systems let the business owner test their core concepts and management structure in the actual marketplace. Developing a Certified Business Model is the first step in the franchise process and is used as a systematic approach to starting and growing business ventures in the 21st Century. The Certified Business Model is a more predictable method for growing a business, and that is why it is preferred by angel investors, venture capitalists, banks and other lending institutions.

The major advantage of the team focused business development process is the attachment of business development teams and third party verifying organizations that can provide network support to business and franchise model owners before and after funding. Economic growth in the new global marketplace requires that business owners secure a niche market with limited competition.

Once a company has a general business model plan it can apply for a code guide number either as a home based business or a micro-business enterprise, by using a third party verifying organization that can assign a Home Business Identity Classification (HBIC) and Micro Business Trade Classification (MBTC) and the Early Stage Franchise Classification (ESFC) code guide numbers. These numbers are assigned to new and existing business ventures. This private numbering system provides order on the exchange, thereby allowing a company to interact with each other worldwide. A code guide number is assigned to a category with similar business ventures, thereby, giving new concepts an identity before they are fully developed. The Counselors, teachers and consultants who enroll in our entrepreneurial focused institute will learn the Modern American Entrepreneurship Philosophy, allowing them to help locate and train the next generation of entrepreneurs.

On the Internet there are many equity capital databases for angel investors. High-net worth angel investors join these networks to gain access to emerging growth companies and search for the Next Big Thing, such as YouTube that sold for 1.2 billion dollars.

Private Equity Finance
Private equity finance is an asset class that consists of an equity stake in companies that are not traded on a public stock exchange such as: the New York Stock Exchange. At the end of 2010, the private equity market had a total of $2.4 trillion dollars under management and more than $1 trillion available for investments, which was 40% of overall assets under management. This was a result of high fund raising volumes between 2006 and 2008. It

could take another three years to invest the current volume of un-invested capital targeted for buyouts and other ventures.

Bloomberg Businessweek has called private equity a rebranding of leveraged buyout firms after the 1980s. Among the most common investment strategies in private equity are: leveraged buyouts, venture capital, growth capital, distressed investments, and mezzanine capital. In a typical leveraged buyout transaction, a private equity firm buys majority control of an existing or mature firm. A leveraged buyout is when another company acquisitions someone's company using a significant amount of borrowed money (bonds or loans) to meet the cost of acquisition. The purpose of leveraged buyouts is to allow companies to make large acquisitions without having to commit a lot of capital. This is distinct from a venture capital or growth capital investment, in which the investors (typically venture capital firms or angel investors) invest in early stage or emerging companies, of which they rarely obtain majority control.

Equity Capital for Startups
A private equity investment is generally made by angel investors, private equity firms, or venture capital firms. Each of these categories of investors has their own set of goals, preferences and investment strategies. Private equity investors are involved in investing in privately held companies. Private equity is also often grouped into a broader category called private capital, which is generally used to describe capital support for a long-term, illiquid investment strategy. Private equity investors that are affiliated with the Equity Capital Access Network invest directly into private companies with certified business models and/or franchises.

The Equity Capital Access Network is an active part of the Franchise Incubator Accelerator, which provides access to crowd funding donations, business formation grants, and equity capital. The business formation stage is a necessary step for entrepreneurs and business owners with new ventures that want to pursue equity capital, once a formation model is complete.

Electronic Wall Street Showcase

The Electronic Wall Street showcase high growth ventures that uses our equity funding platform. This investment project showcases only highlight small business ventures with certified business and franchise models. Franchises are highlighted on Electronic Wall Street are part of a major business development and funding program. These funding packages include; virtual business development incubators, business model plan templates and access to Equity and Venture Capital SourceBanks. Each business owner that is accepted are assigned to a business development team that can provide assistance them 24/7 or when needed. The Franchise Stock Exchange allows investors to bid on these investment opportunities over a fix period of time.

VII. Virtual Franchise Business Model

Early Stage Franchising is a private sector initiative within the traditional franchise industry that uses special institutions to provide continues development and support to the franchise business systems it develops. Early Stage Franchising is the process from which the Virtual Business Model is derived. In order to be considered a Virtual Business Model the enterprise must perform 90% of its business functions electronically.

An Early Stage Franchise Model is built on a business development and support platform, so that it can be changed and updated rapidly when needed. These franchises are developed in two distinct stages, the first is the business formation model stage and the second is the franchise model development stage. In each market where early stage franchises are sold there is a Private Sector Business Infrastructure established to support it. When an Early Stage Franchise is first launched it is assigned a business development and support team, to handle the constant changes it will face when entering the new global marketplace. The Virtual Business Franchise is unique because of its global market reach, on the day it is officially launched.

Virtual Business Franchise

A Virtual Business Franchise is planned from the start. The development process for a Virtual Business Model starts in a business formation Incubator at the embryonic stage of a new business idea, long before it is developed into a full-service franchise. Unlike, the traditional franchise startup that because successfully from trial and error. This business franchise system starts as an Early Stage Franchise in a Franchise Incubator Accelerator. The Early Stage Franchise Association (ESFA) maintains the integrity of the Virtual Business Franchise through it model certification program.

The Virtual Business Franchise combines the chain store outlet structure with the franchise territory structures this allows it to use a multi-unit franchising marketing strategy. This expansion structure that let it offer undeveloped franchise territories to investors on the Early Stage Franchise Investment Exchange. The combining of these two marketing structures allows the Virtual Business Franchise to grow more rapidly in the global marketplace.

A Virtual Business Franchise is a Dual-Unit Franchise System that may sell or leases both physical and virtual locations as a single territory. The Dual-Unit Franchise System is a physical outlet that is surrounded by Virtual Franchise Territories, this allow a Master Franchisee to buy the Multi-Unit Franchise Market as part of the purchase of Virtual Franchise Territory a well.

The Virtual Business Franchise is unique because of its global market reach the day it is launched. Before a Virtual Business Model or Franchise is sold to investors it is certified by the Early Stage Franchise Association. The different between a Virtual Business Franchise and a traditional franchise is a traditional franchise model uses physical landmark including land surveys to determine the location of the business. Virtual Business Franchises use zip codes, email addresses, cell and home phone numbers to identify their customer base.

A Virtual Business Franchise include an advance order tracking system that has the ability to record all sells in virtual territories in real time. It gives Virtual Territory Investors up-to-date accounting on all products or services sold in their territory 24/7. It gives real-time updates to the company's inventory control at the center where tracking system operations and allocate deliveries where needed. Every time an order is originated and sold in a Virtual Franchise Territory the investor get a percentage of the sell at a rate agreed upon in Territory Lease Agreement for the Virtual Franchise Territory. When Virtual Franchise Territory is added to the traditional franchise industry it will make it possible to offer both physical and virtual territories to developed and undeveloped franchise territories for a selected franchise business system.

When the territory purchased is large enough for additional franchise outlets, they can sell the undeveloped franchise territory to other Investors. This franchise combines the traditional franchise model with multi-unit franchising marketing for both the physical and virtual franchise territory. They may also sell virtual territory agreements without seeking permission from the Franchisor or the Master Franchisee. What type of territory agreement is used depends on the product or service offered and what is allowed by government agencies for a particular type of franchise. The selling or leasing of virtual franchise territory is handled exclusively on the Early Stage Franchise Investment Exchange. It is the exclusive provider of the Dual-Unit Franchise that allows it to buy, sell and lease exclusively on FranchiseStockExchange.Com.

Partial Virtual Business Model

Existing chain stores owners are quickly creating outlets on the Internet. Two of the most recent were Staple the office supply chain that is closing 225 stores and Home Depot, the home building supply center announced that it is no longer opening any new stores in physical building. Home Depot grew their revenue in the past by blanketing the U.S. with large box stores. Today they are switching to online stores because shopper-habits have change considerable in the age of the Internet.

Home Depot is investing $1.5 billion dollars in online "Virtual Stores". Staples closed 40 stores in 2013 and will closes 225 additional stores in 2014, so says its management. There brick and mortar stores lost revenue of 7% while their online revenue rose 10%. Staple management said by closing there brick and mortar stores, they would save an additional $500 million dollars in overhead. Radio Shack was another largest electronic retailer that closed 1100 stores. Big box stores are rapidly become a thing of the past and that include shopping malls.

Virtual Business Franchise Rules

Early Stage Franchising is a new field in the traditional franchise industry and home to the "Virtual Business Franchise", the billion dollar startup and the Franchise Incubator Accelerator that convert certified business models into franchises in months instead of years. Early Stage Franchising is a private sector initiative that need special institutions to provide continues development and support through a special team of consultants that handle the constant changes it will face when entering the new marketplace.

According, to industry research and the World Bank, Concept funding generated $5.1 billion in funding transactions in 2013 and will surpass $300 billion in funding transactions by 2025. There are more than 50 million new unaccredited investors entering the private equity market after Title III of the Jobs Act is implemented, there could be an increase of 30% to 40% in business owners that use some form of Concept funding that include: Crowd Funding Donations, Business Formation Grants, Equity and Venture Capital.

Concept Starter Enterprises specializes in the development and management of virtual business franchises and is the exclusive provider of special programs and services needed for the business formation and development models that precede the Virtual Business Franchise.

• The Virtual Business Franchise has a double level territory, one for virtual and the other for physical locations. The Virtual Franchise Territory maybe sold on the Early Stage Franchise Investment Exchange separately.

• When an independent franchise outlet is open the franchisee has the first option to buy back the Virtual Franchise Territory at the current market price which factor in past earning from the virtual territory

• The Virtual Business Franchise is unique because of its global market reach the day it is launched. Before a Virtual Business Model or Franchise is sold to unaccredited investors it is certified by the Early Stage Franchise Association (ESFA).

• The different between a Virtual Business Franchise and a traditional franchise is a traditional model uses physical landmark including land surveys to determine the location of the business. Virtual Business Franchises use zip codes, email addresses, cell and home phone numbers to identify their customer base.

• Early Stage Franchising has a predictable business structure that allows investors to easily follow the growth of the new ventures they invest in.

• This franchise combines the traditional franchise model with multi-unit marketing to allow for the selling of both the physical and virtual franchise territory.

• When the territory purchased is large enough for additional franchise outlets, they can sell the undeveloped franchise territory to a potential Virtual Territory Investors.

• They may also sell virtual territory agreements without seeing permission from the Franchisor or the Master Franchisee.

What type of territory agreement is used depends on the product or service offered and what is allowed by government agencies for a particular type of franchise

• A Virtual Business Franchise is a Dual-Unit Franchise System that may sell or leases both the physical and virtual locations of to authorized territory or for independent franchise outlets including undeveloped territory parcels.

• The Dual-Unit Franchise System is a physical outlet that is surrounded by Virtual Franchise Territories.

• A Master Franchisee that buys a Multi-Unit Franchise Marketing as part of their purchase of franchise territories may be sold as a Virtual Franchise Territory separately.

• The selling or leasing of virtual franchise territories is handled exclusively on the Early Stage Franchise Investment Exchange. It is the exclusive provider of the Dual-Unit Franchise that allows it to buy, sell and lease exclusively on FranchiseStockExchange.Com.

• Every time an order is originated in Virtual Franchise Territory with an owner/investor, they will get a small percentage of the sell at a rate that was predetermined in advance of the sales or lease of the Virtual Franchise Territory.

• A Virtual Business Franchise is an advance order tracking system that comes with the ability to record all sells in virtual territories in real time. It gives Virtual Investors up-to-date accounting on all products or services sold in their territory 24/7. It gives real-time updates to the company's inventory control center where operations allocate delivery and other needed services to all areas of the company.

- When Virtual Franchise Territory is added to the traditional franchise industry it will make it possible to offer both physical and virtual territories to developed and undeveloped franchise territory for selected franchise business systems.

Virtual Franchise Territory

The Virtual Business Franchise is the highest level business system in franchising and can be started at the embryonic stage of a new business idea. This franchise combines the traditional franchise model with the multi-unit franchise marketing system. This system will allow for the selling of both the physical and virtual franchise territories. When the territory purchased is large enough for additional franchise outlets, they can sell the undeveloped franchise territory to potential Virtual Territory Investors.

We are living in the Era of the "Billion Dollar Startup" whether you are a business owner or an investor that is new to private equity investing, this could be the best time to enter the field of franchising. In this Era a million dollars no longer define being rich it merely define the starting point.

Figure #1

Virtual Business Franchise
Funding Forward Chart

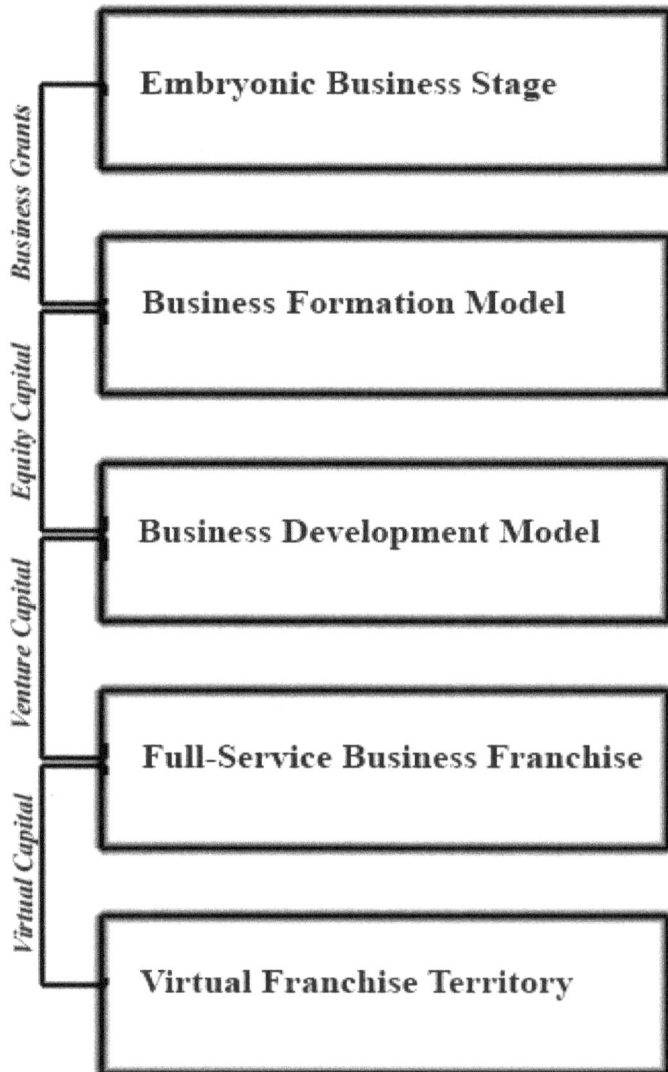

Business Grants

Embryonic Business Stage

Equity Capital

Business Formation Model

Business Development Model

Venture Capital

Full-Service Business Franchise

Virtual Capital

Virtual Franchise Territory

Every time an order is originate in a Virtual Franchise Territory the owner/investor gets a small percentage of the sell, at a rate that is predetermined in advance of the sales or lease in the Virtual Franchise Territory. A Virtual Business Franchise is an advance system that comes with the ability to track and record all sells in virtual territories in real time. It gives the Virtual Investor up-to-date accounting on all products or services sold in their territory 24/7.

In January 2002, Papa John's became the first national pizza chain to make online ordering available to all of its U.S. customers. Most other national chains subsequently added online ordering to their services. On July 10, 2004, Papa John's controlled an estimated 6.6 percent of the market, according to Technomic, a food service industry research and consulting firm. Papa John's is credited with developing an advanced resource control infrastructure in the fast food industry. Sources stated their centralized network is linked via fiber optic cables to national headquarters. It gives real-time updates to the company's inventory control center where operations allocate delivery and other needed services to all areas of the company.

Dual-Unit Franchise System

A Virtual Business Franchise is a Dual-Unit Franchise System that sell and/or lease both physical and virtual locations to authorized territories for independent outlets including undeveloped franchise territory parcels. The Dual-Unit Franchise System is a physical outlet that is surrounded by Virtual Franchise Territories. This is done when the core product is a physical item. The Dual-Unit Franchise System was first use by CondoFran® an Affordable Condominium Apartment Conversion Service. It offered two systems, one for residential and another for commercial properties.

Master Franchisees

Master Franchisees have exclusive marketing rights over territories as small as a town and/or as large as a county. A Master Franchisee that buys a franchise with a multi-unit franchise marketing agreement may sell the Virtual Franchise Territory separately. The selling or leasing of virtual franchise territories is handled exclusively on the Early Stage Franchise Investment Exchange. It is the exclusive provider of the Dual-Unit Franchise that allow for buying, selling and leasing of virtual territory agreements in developed and undeveloped territories exclusively through FranchiseStockExchange.Com.

Franchise territories are privately owned, and are authorized to sell independent franchise outlet in their territories. Once territories are open with a sufficient number of business and support associates in place, they recruit independent and major services providers to assist them in servicing new entrepreneurs.

Multi-Unit Franchising

The world's markets are too large to open a single franchise outlet one at a time. Multi-unit franchising is a new marketing alternative that has emerged for business owners with franchise business systems that want to achieve national and international market saturation in their lifetimes. Multi-unit franchising is a business marketing phenomenon that is being lead by a new entrepreneurial class of business owners; Rudy Lewis called them "Super-Entrepreneurs", in his book that shares the same name. These special entrepreneurs work in ventures that they didn't necessarily start. In most cases, they didn't create the core franchise system or the brand they are so successful in.

In recent years the concept of multi-unit franchising has become the preferred method of developing franchise territories. The success of multi-unit franchising is due to options given to the franchisee by the franchisor that allows them to start more than one franchise in a designated territory.

In 2008, FRANdata, a franchise industry research firm conducted a survey and found that more than 50% of all franchises sold in the United States were sold through multi-unit franchising. The success of multi-unit franchising is due to options given to franchisees by franchisors that allow them to start more than one franchise in a designated territory.

Some of America's top companies include; Domino Pizza, Subway Sandwich and Kentucky Fried Chicken, Jiffylube, Churches Chicken, Dunkin Donuts, and Aaron's Rental to name a few that are using multi-franchising to grow their brand. Three of the best known Multi-Unit leaders are Patrick Doyle, CEO of Domino Pizza, Herman Cain, the former republican presidential candidate and former President & CEO of Godfather's Pizza. Sean Touey whose real life story inspired the book and movie, "The Blind Side", owns more than 70 Pizza Hut Restaurants.

The Multi-Unit Franchise System is bringing economic changes to the world through multi and dual unit franchise and the exclusive territories they cover. The United States' private sector is now being lead by a new entrepreneurial class of super-entrepreneurs that use multi-unit franchising to expand their business brand globally.

Multi-unit franchising is a fast growth business system that can provide entrance level jobs for the masses, while offering management and ownership opportunities to others. Today, more and more people are embracing this new marketing expansion strategy, which they believe can provide a new future for their children who choose the right brands. Pre-Employment Leadership Screening Program is a placement service for the multi-unit franchise business system. The pre-employment program includes the following: Work-to-own franchise seminars & workshops, and secondary business and career training options.

Multi-unit franchising has brought about a new type of equity capital formation in addition to franchise stock being purchased and sold on the Franchise Stock Exchange. Multi-unit franchise territory will also be bought and sold on the Franchise Stock Exchange. The Franchise Stock Exchange is a place where qualified investors and franchise system owners come to fund their new and expanding franchise territories. Only, territories with a predetermine number of outlets may be sold on the exchange. Angel investors and venture capital firms also use the FSE to invest in new franchise systems with territory expansion strategies.

In recent years the concept of multi-unit franchising has become the preferred method of developing franchise territories. The United States private sector is now being lead by a new entrepreneurial class of Super-entrepreneurs that use multi-unit franchising to expand their business brand globally. Multi-unit franchising provides the best environment for this new class of entrepreneurs to grow. The Franchise Stock Exchange will allow small investors to participate in the early stage funding period for franchise business systems that are established and need funds to grow.

Certified business models & franchises are the new starting point for entrepreneurs who want to own their own business ventures. Certified business and franchise models are built on growth and development platforms by a business development team that is assigned to each project that's being certified, thereby been available to the business owner when needed. This allows team members to share in the business concept knowledge from the beginning until the enterprise is funded.

Brazilians now uses franchising as a business starting point, since starting a business from scratch is so difficult in Brazil. The franchise model has emerged as the simplest and safest way to own a small business for new entrepreneurs. According to the Brazilian Association of Franchising, between 2002 and 2010 the number of Brazilians age 18 to 24 became entrepreneurs, which was a rise of 74% according to the Global Entrepreneurship Monitor. In the past 10 years, franchising in Brazil has been growing by an average of between 10% and 13% annually according to the association.

Small business owners are the driving force behind the United States Economy and the leading creators of new jobs. Small businesses account for more than 70% of all new jobs created in the United States during the past 15 years. However, statistics show that these small businesses have a short life span, shorter than 5 years. Where traditional small business ventures fall short, franchise models started during that same period have a more than 90% success rate. Therefore, entrepreneurs that start franchises can provide longer term job security for those who go to work for them, thereby bringing new management and ownership opportunities to the Modern American Workforce.

The success of this type of the Multi-Unit Franchise Fast Track Leadership Management Program has the potential to change the relationship between employees and employers forever.

VIII. Small & Medium Enterprises

Small & Medium size Enterprises (SMEs) is a new classification for the world's largest business group. Two-thirds of the world's businesses are Small & Medium size Enterprises and they account for 70% of all new jobs created. The term "SME" is used by international organizations such as; the European Union (EU), World Bank, United Nations and the World Trade Organization (WTO) to describe both business investments and international trade activities. SME is used for companies whose personnel numbers fall below certain limits set by them. The United States defined a Small & Medium Enterprise as a business venture with less than 500 employees.

Following are the world's top five public stock exchanges:
1) The New York Stock Exchange is largest stock exchange in the world by both market capitalization and trade value. The holding company created by the combination of NYSE Group, Inc. and Euronext, it is headquartered in New York City. The NYSE featuring more than 8000 listed issues includes 90% of the Dow Jones Industrial Average and 82% of the S&P 500 stock market indexes volume.

2) The NASDAQ is the secondary largest stock exchange in the world by aggregate market capitalization with 2,292 companies which are separated into two sections, the first is for large companies, the second section is for mid-sized companies.

3) Tokyo Stock Exchange in Japan is the third largest stock exchange in the world. It had 2,292 listed companies with a combined market capitalization of US$4.09 trillion dollars.

4) The London Stock Exchange is the fourth-largest stock exchange Located in the City of London it is the oldest and fourth-largest stock exchange in the world. The Exchange was founded in

1801 and its current premises are situated in Paternoster Square close to St Paul's Cathedral. It is the most international of all the world's stock exchanges, with around 3,000 companies from over 70 countries admitted to trade on its markets.

5) Hong Kong Stock Exchange is the world's 5th largest stock market by market capitalization and one of the two stock exchanges operating independently in the People's Republic of China. In 2014, China combined the stock markets of Shanghai with Hong Kong, thereby creating the fifth largest public stock exchange in the world. London, England is now considered the home of the Alternative Investment Market (AIM) for Small & Medium Enterprise Investment Exchanges. In other countries Small & Medium Enterprise Investment Exchanges are being attached to largest public stock exchanges, in London England, Tokyo, Japan, Mumbai, India, Johannesburg, South Africa, Shanghai, China and other cities, as sub-exchanges.

AIM was established in London is 2005, thereby making it one of the largest in the world. Currently, there are more than 3,000 companies enrolled in AIM compared to China where they are simply known as over the counter stock. China had only 200 companies in their SMEs Investment Exchanges in 2013. In 2014 China combine the stock markets of Shanghai with Hong Kong, thereby creating one of the largest public stock markets in world. Today, the Shenzhen market is the home of China's SME Investment Exchange for start-up companies and small and medium-sized enterprises. China is expected to soon launch a Shenzhen-Hong Kong Stock Exchange. Shenzhen China is a major city in Southern China's Guangdong Province.

In India, Small and Medium size Enterprise Exchanges are established in the cities of Mumbai and Bombay. In London and South African they are known as the Alternative Investment-Market. Since, SME Investment Exchanges are being established in countries with 2/3 the worldwide population. SMEs Investment Exchanges will someday be larger than all the existing public stock exchanges in London, Tokyo, New York and other cities combined. The Global Cities Management is rewriting the words for "Small and Medium size Enterprises SMEs" while keeping the definition. The Global Cities Management Organization will recognize a new phase as the American version called: "Small & Medium Enterprises. The Early Stage Franchise Investment Exchange is a major part of a Private Sector Business Infrastructure that is being established in cities by the Global Cities Management Organization. In the United States a Private Sector Business Infrastructure include the Early Stage Franchise Investment Exchange, Electronic Wall Street, the EquityStakeExchange.Com and the FranchiseStockExchange.Com.

Global Cities Management (GCM) is made-up of partnerships that manage authorized Global Cities Projects in enrolled cities. Global Cities Management may reserve up to a 5% stake of each first round funding for Donor Contributors that award business formation grants to formation projects as seed money in cities where a management partnership is being formed. When unaccredited investors are allowed to invest in small & medium size enterprises in the United States, these investment exchanges will be attached to public stock exchanges.

Global Cities Management is building a private sector business investment exchange for Small & Medium Enterprises. This SME Investment Exchange specializes in Early Stage Franchising. The Early Stage Franchise Investment Exchange will have branches in major cities around the world where more than 5 billion people will live by 2030, thereby, making a selected city a financial center that will attract new investors to enrolled cities. SME Investment Exchanges are coming to America, how you see your company fitting into this new market. Thanks, to Title III of the Jobs Act that allow ordinary people to invest in a global franchise brand of their choice. It is estimated that 51 thousand non-accredited investors will enter the US market, thereby causing an economic boom.

Cities with the right type of private sector business infrastructure will have fast growth in both their public and private sectors. However, they will need private sector business infrastructures that can help it change from a domestic city into a Global City. Today, when you buy a stake in a Global Cities Project you are participating in a major shift in investment opportunities being created in cities. Federal and states government agencies usually don't get directly involve in private equity investing; therefore, it is up to business owners, new entrepreneurs and private investors living in these cities to establish and manage their own business investment activities.

With the increase in growth expected in large U.S. cities, local city officials can no longer wait for manufacturing plants to return and create jobs for their communities. Today, a city can establish a strong private sector that will generate jobs by creating new business ventures, starting from the embryonic stage of new business ideas to franchise business systems.

Private Sector Business Infrastructure

In today's fast paced economy small business owners need access to business and support professionals that can help them to start and/or grow their business ventures. The world currently has two economies, one old, and the other new. The old economy depended heavily on debt financing by banks and other lending institutions. Small business owners operating in the new economy want rapid growth, therefore, they prefer equity capital to debt financing for building their high growth companies.

The Private Sector Business Infrastructure in cities includes Concept Funding access to Small & Medium Enterprises which include crowd funding donations, business formation grants, equity and venture capital. SMEs can use Global City Projects to connect to other cities both domestic and foreign. This is a low cost way to expand a business through a membership network that includes business owners and private investors. This new business infrastructure will allow ordinary people to own an equity stake their cities. Concept Starter Enterprises is committed to giving non-accredited investors an opportunity to share in the growth of each city they enroll. In the United States the Private Sector Business Infrastructure, include the Early Stage Franchise Investment Exchange, Electronic Wall Street, the EquityStakeExchange.Com and the FranchiseStockExchange.Com.

MicroBusiness Enterprises

In the late 90s the Small Business Administration (SBA) recognized a new group of small businesses called; "MicroBusinesses". MicroBusiness is a new Style of American Entrepreneurship that's spreading rapidly around the world. These small & home based business owners are distinguished by having no paid employees.

MicroBusiness owners outsource work to other like minded entrepreneurs in a Virtual Assembly Line spanning the globe. In the United States their numbers reached more than 25 million in 2007 with an annual growth rate of 7.3%. According to government data they generated annual revenues of more than $1 trillion dollars. MicroBusiness models and franchises offer some of the leading business and training opportunities for people who want to be self-employed. It is hard to create next generation business enterprises when there is no appropriate system used to identify and categorize MicroBusiness owners.

Business Code Guide Numbers

Certified business models are assigned private business trade group numbers. Only certified business models may carry their own private BTG numbers. The Certified Business Model will become an even more viable option when selected equity capital access sources identify a new class of investors that will consider these models exclusively. At the beginning of this model program the entrepreneur needs to be able to select the type of business field the venture use such as: a Standard Industrial Classification (SIC), this number is used by government agencies. The Micro-Business Trade Classification (MBTC), the Early Stage Franchise Classification (ESIC) and the Home Business Identity Classification, (HBIC) are private sector code guide numbers.

Entrepreneurs who want to start a new business venture or expand an existing one beyond their local market, the Business Development Team can provide them with a Business Model Plan document that will raise your investment score, which is necessary when applying for investment capital. Use our Business Model Plan template to produce a document online or a copy that can be presented to leading institutions and private investors. Business Model Plan is an online document that can be presented for funding and other management projects. Leading financial institutions prefer Business Model Plans, because of the network support you can receive from a Business Development Team before and after funding.

Micro-Business Trade Classification

The Micro-Business Trade Classification allows small business trends to be monitored worldwide. This system allows new business types to be detected in an industry when they first come into existence. This allows all existing members in the network to become potential trading partners. The Business Trade Group is at the heart of this new global marketing strategy and is used by business owners who are expanding beyond their local markets.

The Business Trade Group is a new classification system for small & medium size enterprises. It categorizes similar business both nationally and internationally. A newly established Business Trade Group includes a Business Trade Organization (BTO). The BTO uses an advanced association structure to group similar business trade groups together. The business trade group is used to identity both small and home-based businesses in a Micro-Business Enterprise System.

Business trade groups place business enterprise in a category with similar businesses nationally. Only the National Association of Home Based Businesses (NAHBB), Micro-Business Enterprise Association (MBEA) and the Early Stage Franchise Association (ESFA) may assigned Business Trade Groups to new business new business categories. This classification will let the small business owners know where their enterprise fit into a group. If there is no trade group for your type of enterprise, the MBEA will create a special BTG category for the product or service you provide. After evaluation, new members are allowed to join a Business Marketing Circle. A Business Marketing Circle is made-up of businesses that offer a one-of-kind product or service. These businesses are allowed to jointly target niche groups. The Business Marketing Circle is the beginning of the Infinity Marketing System where a business can grow without limitations.

Business Verifying Organizations

The Franchise Incubator Accelerator shortens the time between conception and when the venture reaches the marketplace. All accepted projects begin with a Business Model Plan that is used to build a Certified Business Model that can be developed into a franchise. Certified Business Models and Franchises are built in Virtual Business Development Incubators and tested in the actual marketplace by 3rd party verifying organizations that include the National Association of Home Based Businesses the Micro-

Business Enterprise Association and the Early Stage Franchise Association. These two organizations have business developers and consultants attached that can assist business owners before and after funding.

IX.   Early Stage Investment Market

The Early Stage Investment Market is a private sector initiative with indirect government participation. However, this new investment market is wholly owned and managed by entrepreneurs in the private sector. The Early Stage Investment Market represents the first stage in the business model formation and equity funding process.

The Small Business Investment Act of 1958 was the first step the federal government took to professionally manage the private equity and venture capital industry. This act officially allowed the SBA to license private "Small Business Investment Companies" (SBICs) to help with financing and managing small entrepreneurial businesses in the United States. The passage of the Small Business Investment Act of 1958 by the federal government was an important incentive for would-be venture capital organizations. When the Small Business Administration first launched the SBIC program it was to fill a gap in the investment market now private equity investing has become the market. The act provided venture capital firms structured either as SBICs or Minority Enterprise Small Business Investment Companies (MESBICs) access to federal funds which could be leveraged at a ratio of up to 4:1 against privately raised investment funds. The SBIC program had its highest ever year in Fiscal Year 2010.

Startup America Intuitive

The United States is the first country to establish the condition for an Early Stage Investment Market for startups by authorizing the first Early Stage Small Business Investment Company (ESSBIC) with a mandate to invest in early stage business ventures without a track record of earnings.

In 2011, the White House announced the "Startup America Initiative" to accelerate entrepreneurship. They started this imitative by calling a Startup America Conference to celebrate entrepreneurship and inspire them to start new ventures throughout the nation. The conference attendees included business and social leaders from corporations, universities, foundations and other public & private institutions. The White House Initiative called on a wide verity of federal agencies to dramatically increase their assistance to help entrepreneur's success. The President's initiative called for the forming of new public and private sector investment partnerships with American's Entrepreneurs.

In order to implement these changes, President Obama ordered his administration to officially implement government initiatives to challenge the private sector with assistance from the government and other public sector programs. This was followed by the signing of Title III of the Jobs Act, on April 5, 2012 that allows non-accredited investors to invest in early stage startup for the first times, since the 1930s. Before, the law you had to be an accredited investor, with a net-worth over $1 million dollars to invest in small business ventures.

Today, crowd funding donors are given millions of dollars in seed funding donations to entrepreneurial inspired projects and other innovative business and social ideas. There are crowd funding websites popping up all over with no regulations to guide them, since the law that was allowing non-accredited investors to invest in early stage startups have not been implemented yet.

President Obama's national business strategy for achieving sustainable growth and quality jobs is to encourage entrepreneur to establish startups business ventures. This will play a critical role in job creation across the country. Entrepreneurs that start new business ventures that create the lion's share of new jobs in every industry. Moreover, the White House Initiative called on entrepreneurs and others to invest in clean energy technology, medicine, advanced manufacturing, information technology, that can help build new industries for the 21st century, and solve some of our toughest global challenges.

On February 17, 2015 the Small Business Administration (SBA) began evaluating Early Stage Fund Managers for a new type of Small Business Investment Company (SBIC), the "Early Stage Small Business Investment Company (ESSBIC)". This new private/public investment company will specialize in startups with no history of earning.

In order to qualify for an SBA licensed to operate an ESSBIC the selected Early Stage Fund Manager must have a minimum of $20 million dollars in regulatory capital to invest. An approved fund must invest at least 50 percent of investment dollars in "early stage small businesses" defined as those never having achieved positive cash flow from operations in any fiscal year before the year of investment. The SBA will provide these newly licensed funds up to a 2:1 match to private capital raised by these funds, partnering with private investors to target "impact" investments.

SBA will also commit $1 billion dollars to those with funds that invest growth capital in companies located in underserved communities, such as inner cities. This will include investing in economically distressed areas as well as those companies in emerging sectors such as clean energy, "the directive said". It also said that the stated goals of this program is to bring the wealth of startups to transformative innovations to market, and also play a critical role in job creation across the United States.

The SBA will continue to license applicants at least through fiscal year 2016. This new SBA program will officially begin the era of the Early Stage Investor (ESI). The ESP Investment Exchange is asking other private sector funding group to join this SBA effort and expand it to other cities throughout the world by establishing private sector business infrastructure projects in other cities with the same types of funders from both the public and private sector. With these new funding source from the SBA and others, in the coming years we estimate a funding preference shift of 30% to 40% of all new business startups to some form of Concept Funding that include: crowd funding donations, business formation grants, equity and/or venture capital.

Private Equity Market for Startups

The American Free Market System is finally allowing equity capital investments from non-accredited investors for the first time, since the 1930s. Title III of the Jobs Act establishes the conditions for the Private Equity Market, for early stage start-ups. Before the new law passed, there were no private equity investment exchanges for early stage start-ups in the United States, were the public could invest. This new law will accelerate the growth of small businesses by allowing them to raise equity capital directly from the general public. This new law will also make it possible to fund new start-up ventures in the concept formation stage. There are two types of concept funding methods used at this stage of growth. The first is capital raised for businesses in the formation stage, and the second is equity capital for existing ventures with business model plans.

Raising capital in the business formation stage can take the form of crowd funding donations or business formation grants, both of these sources of funds offered no actual stake in a company or any say in where and how the funds are being used. There are no business plans requirements to receive crowd funding donations on many of the current websites.

The old philosophy of starting a business by trial and error has given way to a virtual formation platform that provides access to equity capital for those that build a successful Business Formation Model. A Business Model Plan is presented to the investor before equity capital funding is made available to owners of new or existing business ventures.

The Small Business Network (SBN) management policy is that it is easier to build a business structure right the first time, than to restructure it to fit the needs of private investors the second time. A business owner that uses a Business Formation Platform to seek equity or venture capital for development and growth will automatically be placed on a fast track development platform that can convert a Certified Business Model into a franchise in months instead of years. Business owners that choose the fast track development path must be able to write a comprehensive Business Model Plan. This Business Model Plan will be developed and tested in the actual marketplace by a third party verifying organization.

Small Business Investment Company

The USA Small Business Administration (SBA begin the era of the Early Stage Investor (ESI), when it began evaluating Early Stage Fund Managers in February 2015 for a new type of "Early Stage Small Business Investment Company (ESSBIC). This private/public investment company specializes in startups with no history of earning. For members in the Early Stage Franchise Industry, these investment companies are known simply as, an "Early Stage Investment Company (ESIC)".

These recent initiatives by the U.S. government will have a major impact on how small business will start and grow in the future. This will mark the ended of the trial and error method of starting and growing a business and the beginning of a startup revolution where early stage ventures are well funding and are built by business development teams instead of a single entrepreneur. These new changes are not occurring in a vacuum, this is the era of the billion dollar startup, where private investors are pouring 100s of millions of dollars into startup ventures.

The USA Small Business Administration (SBA) is the first U.S. government agency to recognize the era of the Early Stage Investor (ESI). This program also officially launched the Early Stage Business Industry. This lays the groundwork for an Equity Stake Exchange for early stage startups that could be larger than all of today's public stock exchanges combined.

Today there are two types of Early Stage Investment Companies (ESICs), the first is a public/private investment company that was first authorized by the Small Business Administration in 2015, and these ESICs were called Early Stage Small Business Investment Companies. The others are originated in the private sector and are called: the Early Stage Investment Companies, they are exclusive owned and managed by private owner(s). These ESICs have no government funding sources. The Early Stage Investment Company also invest in early stage business ventures with no history of earning, however, there are not mandates that is do so.

The Early Stage Franchise Association has the sole authority to certify ESICs or early stage investors that are allowed to operate in the ESP Investment Exchange. The mission of the Early Stage Investment Company is to invest in business ventures form the embryonic stage of a new idea. This is also the market that official begin the new Small & Medium size Enterprise Stock Exchange.

Modern Equity Capital Market

The Modern Equity Capital Market in the United States was started more than 80 years ago. It gave rise to financial brokerages, venture capital firms, angel investors and now hedge fund management firms. Today, we live in the era of the Billion

Dollar Startup and where a new investment class has emerged. The Early Stage Investor seeks no investment assurance when they invest in new business ventures with no track record of earning. They get their investment back when the business they invest in is sold or goes public through an Initial Public Offering (IPO).

Early stage investors use Proof of Concept (POC) as their criteria for investing. This new type of investor uses the Business Model Plan and the Investment Scoring System to assist them in determining the Proof of Concept for ventures with previous records of earning. The key to successful investing in the era of the Billion Dollar Startup is finding the right business projects during the embryonic business stage of a business idea.

In the current private equity market there are two major classes of investors; one is the Traditional Private Investor (TPI) and Early Stage Investor (ESI). The Traditional investor's uses "Return on Investment (ROI) as their investing criteria to estimate the value of the ventures they want to invest in. These investors seek investments with a market evaluation that support the owner's asking price of the venture they choose. This type of investor grew out of a time when you had to have a million dollars before you could invest in early stage business ventures.

Traditionally, in the United States an accredited investor with a net worth of at least $1 million dollars to invest in private equity ventures. Once, these programs are fully implemented, there will be an estimated 51 million non-accredited investors eligible to enter the private equity market once, the law is fully implemented, however, this may cause a shortest of quality ventures to invest in. According to industry research and the World Bank, Concept Funding generated $5.1 billion in funding transactions in 2013 and will surpass $300 billion in funding transactions by 2025. SME Investment Exchanges are a viable alternative funding source that small business owners can now access.

Investment Trend Lines

There are two separate trend lines that follow new and existing businesses; we call them the Growth Direction Line and Investment Trend Lines. These lines are parallel to each other in an existing venture and are pointed in the same direction. However, the Investment Trend Line of an Early Stage Business Venture is reversed, one hundred and eighty degrees compared to the Growth Direction Line. Investment Trend Line is used to define two investment strategies, one for traditional investors with existing business ventures and the other for early stage ventures with no history of earning. Traditional Investors use the trend lines to analyze growth using progressive cash flow by following the step-by-step growth of a potential company they want to invest in.

The Investment Trend Line of early stage startups is different from that of an existing franchise business system, especially during the business formation period. The Early Stage Investment Trend Line flows in the opposite direction of the Growth Direction Line because early stage investors want to invest at the most feasible point during the embryonic stage of a new idea, sometime before the Proof of Concept can be determined. Early Stage Investors use Proof of Concept to analyze a new venture they want to invest in. Start-up ventures Growth Direction Line go in the same direction as a traditional venture. The Growth Direction Line follows the same process as the business cycle. *(See the below figure for a clearer view)*

Figure #2

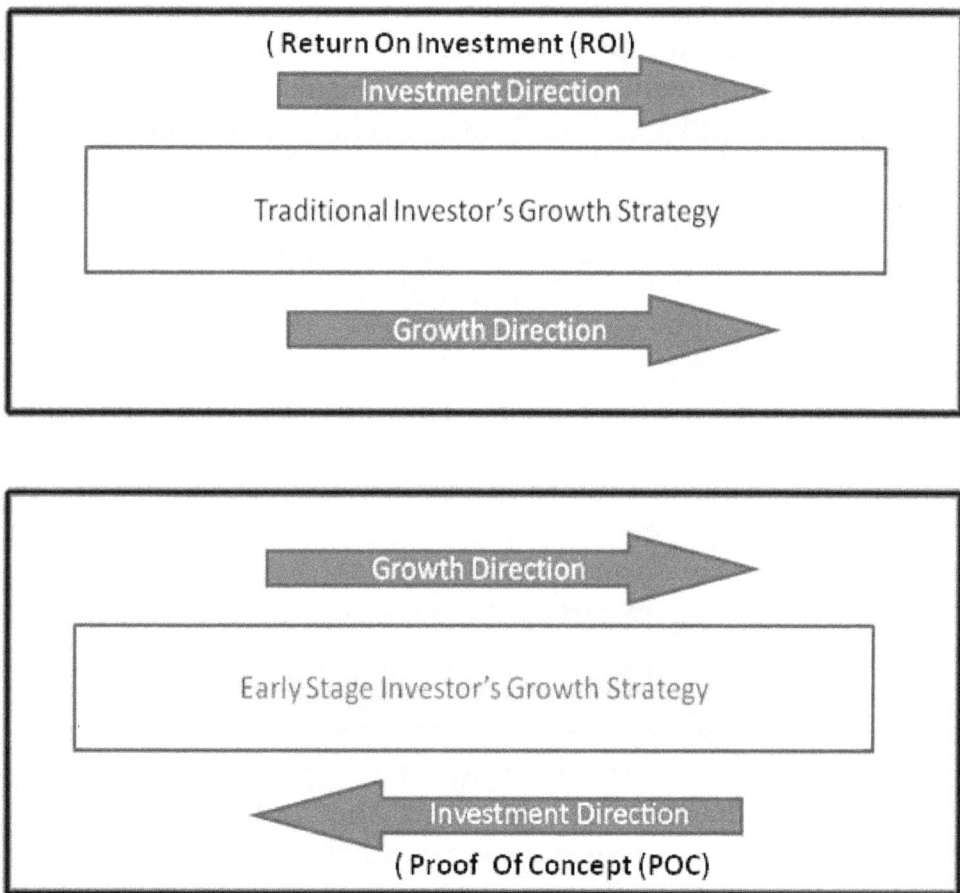

(Return On Investment (ROI)

Investment Direction →

Traditional Investor's Growth Strategy

Growth Direction →

Growth Direction →

Early Stage Investor's Growth Strategy

← Investment Direction

(Proof Of Concept (POC)

Investment Access Provider

Venture capital brokers are investment access providers who can own and manage their own Investment firms. However, they're venture capital brokers until they gain access to a funding source with minimum of ten million dollars to invest. These firms maintain databases of both high net-worth private investors and as well as early stage investors.

An Investment Access Provider can be either a Venture or Equity Capital Broker that specializes in providing equity & venture capital funding access to owners of business models and franchises. This newly authorized professional has been added to the venture capital industry to assist in assigning points to investment opportunities for high net-worth investors. Early Stage Investors use investment access companies to screen investment opportunities with a predetermined scoring range.

Those that qualify can administrate the Investment Scoring System, a new analysis tool used by private investors to evaluate investment opportunities before they invest. These capital access brokers also prepare venture capital funding packages for business owners and others. Private investors use independent firms to screen their investment opportunities, using a predetermined investment scoring range. The Investment Access Provider uses a pre-qualified list of investors based solely on an investment score assigned investment the opportunity at the enrollment process. In order to achieve the goals of the Investment Scoring System, the Certified Business Model Plan must be synonymous with its equity funding goals. The first step for a company that enrolls in an investment access network is to get the highest investment score possible before they contact an angel investor, because most investors ask for a particular scoring range when they sign-up and don't want to be bothered with venture opportunities that don't match their investment portfolios.

Investment Scoring System

The Investment Scoring System allows angel investors to become organized. Each qualified owner that enroll in an equity capital funding program will be allowed to access a pre-qualified list of investors, based on their assigned investment score. The new Investment Scoring System was developed by investment access companies that interviewed angel investors, venture capitalists, experienced entrepreneurs, and owners of high-growth private companies.

Since the introduction of the Investment Scoring System and the Certified Business Model, a more predictable path to acquiring equity funding has emerged. This score provides owners with critical feedback while improving the attractiveness of their business ventures to potential investors. A Certified Business Model is a business venture that has had its core concept tested in the actual marketplace by an authorized third party verifying organization. These business and diversified trade organizations only accept companies that they can assist before and after funding.

The Investment Scoring System measures tangible and intangible assets; such as customer acceptance, market potential, competitive advantage, leading edge technology, market size, niche market share signed deals, intelligent property, and management team experiences. The Investment Scoring System has given rise to a need for certified business models that are built in small business incubators by business development teams. This allows business owners and new entrepreneurs seeking funding to have access to support associates and support professionals that can assist them when needed.

An Investment Scoring Range (ISR) is used by business owners and their Investment Access Providers to meet investor criteria.

This new Investment Scoring System has given business owners seeking funds from private investors, a new way to meet investment criteria. Since the introduction of the Investment Scoring Range and the broad use of the Certified Business Model, new investment access steps have been added to the process.

The Investment Scoring Range saves a business owner time and money while increasing their chances of getting the investment they need. Before the Investment Scoring Range was established, a business owner seeking equity or venture capital had to guess why their venture capital request was rejected. Today, a business owner can have an Investment Scoring Survey conducted by the Investor Access Provider to identify the most important qualities an investor wants before presenting an investment opportunity to investors to choose. Private investors don't want to be bothered with business concepts and ventures that don't match their investment criteria.

When the Investment Scoring Range is combined with the needs of the selected franchise models, a predictable growth path is established for a new privately held company. Certified business models and franchises are assigned the highest investment score and therefore, can be presented to a special class of private investors and venture capitalists. Importantly, the Investment Scoring Range assigned the same scores to certified business and franchise models as it does to high net-worth companies.

The Investment Scoring Range measures companies potential from the investors' perspective. It answers key questions about today's worth as it relates to tomorrow's value. An investment score helps entrepreneurs determine the most important qualities investors are seeking. This lets investment opportunities to be grouped in easy-to-understand categories. The Investment Scoring Range is used by angel investors to determine which opportunities fit their investment criteria. This new investment analyzing tool was developed by private investment access companies that specializing in angel investments. They interviewed angel investors, venture capitalists, presidents of high-growth companies, and experienced entrepreneurs.

Capital Access Score

The Capital Access Score is a new analysis tool used by a new class of private investors to evaluate investment opportunities before they invest. The Capital Access Score helps the business owner to understand how their companies are being analyzed by an investor. The Capital Access Score measures tangible and intangible assets; such as customer acceptance, market potential, competitive advantage, leading edge technology, market size, niche market shares, signed deals, intelligent property, and management team experience. The capital access score takes into consideration key assets that exist in an early stage company that are ignored by banks and other financial institutions. Investment access companies assign a scoring range to each business ventures they evaluate.

The Investment Scoring Range is automatically updated when additional information is provided by the owner, such as; the adding of a management team member, new attraction in the marketplace, new technology added, or other critical factors that could change the effectiveness of the business venture.

A Capital Access Score is used to help new entrepreneurs determine what investors are looking for, plus critical feedback to help improve their venture attractiveness to investors. The scoring also provides investors with a snap shot of a new company's development stage before funding is offered. Investors use these investment scores to get a real time sense of what is the true marketing position in a particular field. The investment score shows what aspects of a company are strong and which aspect need improvements. It also helps the investor determine the chance of success based on the current financial and income status of the company. This scoring system provides business owners with critical feedback that can help them to improve the attractiveness of their business ventures to potential investors. Additionally, it helps a business owner understand how their company is being perceived by potential investors. It's used by investment access providers; to screen potential investments for nigh-net worth private investors.

Once an actual score has been assigned, they can request and upgrade their score from the Investment Access Provider that administered the test. The score takes into consideration key assets that exist in an early stage company that are ignored by banks and other traditional financial institutions. It measures tangibles and intangibles, such as customer acceptance, market potential, competitive advantage, leading edge technology, market sector comparable, signed deals, intellectual property, and management team experience. These are essential questions that need answers when raising money from private Investors. Additionally, it provides the investors with a snap shot of a new company's development stage before funding is offered. Investors use the investment score to get a real time sense of what is the company's true marketing position in a particular field. The investment score shows what aspects of a company are strong and which aspect need improvements. It also helps the investor determine the chance of success based on the current financial and income status of the company.

Selection & Preference Scoring

Concept Starter uses its membership subscriber's base to help Early Stage Investors with the Business Formation Model selection process. During the formation period of a project listed on Concept Starter when seeking business formation grants as seed money, usually over a period of six months. Concept Starter uses this period to compare projects and the public interest in a project during the embryonic stage of a new business venture.

ConceptStarter.Net keeps track of its visitors in Preferred Selection Process that was created for its Investment Scoring System. Each Business Formation Model has a track record kept while it is listed during a six months period on the website. This method of investing is used when an investor is gather information to determine Proof of Concept. This method of selection compares other projects during a stated period of time during the initial funding raising process.

Following are the scoring interest classifications:

- **Public Interest Score (PIS)**
  The Public Interest Score (PIS) is determined by the total number of visitors to a particular project that is listing website.

- **Section Visit Score (SVS)**
  The Section Visit Score (SVS) is created from the total number of visitors to a Business Formation Project with similar profiles.

- **Project Comparison Score (PCS)**
  The Project Comparison Score (PCS) is compiled from the comparison form the same number of visitors to all the other listings during a six months period of time.

- **Donor Contributor Score (DCS)**
  The Donor Contributor Score (DCS) is perhaps the most important score for an Early Stage Investor (ESI) that is seeking to analyze an early stage business venture for the Proof of Concept (POC).

X.   Equity & Venture Capital SourceBanks

A startup venture may require several rounds of financing before it can generate sufficient cash flow to finance its own operations. New entrepreneurs will need funds to support their business formation models before it is funded. Unlike venture capital firms and others that invest in traditional companies with a track record, where investors can review it, a business venture in the embryonic stage of a new business idea has little financial history to review.

Early Stage Investments

An equity investment is created when an investor purchases a share in a legally established business enterprise. Private investors that invest in early stage companies receive higher returns on their investments when they are sold. An equity stake provides direct ownership in a company where the investment is made. Early stage high-growth startups are less risky than public stocks. An equity stake is different from public trading stock and may be harder to sell in a hurry, if you need to liquidate your stake.

A person who holds shares in a company with outstanding equity shares will profit when the company is sold or acquired. Unlike, a public trading company where the value of the stock has very little relationship to the value of the company. The number of outstanding equity shares is linked to the overall worth of a company. When an owner(s) accept outside investments in their company their shares decrease. Share prices increase when the overall value of the company increases and is less venerable to speculation. In the past, equity capital investment was unavailable to ordinary people in the United States because of limits placed on them by states and federal laws that specify the amount of money an individual must have before they could invest.

There are equity capital brokerages attached to serve franchisors with existing franchise business systems and the exclusive territories they cover. The long term goal of Franchise Stock Exchange is to create a liquefied marketplace for franchise business systems with exclusive territories.

The Equity Stake Exchange accepts business ventures in the first funding cycle. This online exchange is used by investors to invest in business formation models before they become a franchise business system. This is a private equity service that concentrates on early stage start-ups. A business owner may choose to raise funds in the formation period of a new business venture without issuing an equity stake in their company. Once the model is built and certified for its readiness to receive equity capital, small investors can invest in it. The Equity Stake Exchange, for early stage start-ups, recognizes business venture in the embryonic business stage of a new idea. However, they can only accept equity or venture capital for them during this period.

The Franchise Incubator Accelerator is a franchise model development service for high growth companies that need equity capital. Business and franchise models that use a Business Model Plan can be tested in the actual marketplace. These certified business and franchise models are built on growth and development platforms where a business development team is assigned to each project that is being certified. Team members make themselves available to business owners when needed. This allows team members to share in the business concept and management knowledge from the beginning until the enterprise is funded.

Today, the Equity Capital Access Network (ECAN) takes much of the guest work out of raising equity capital. Equity & Venture Capital SourceBanks are an important part of the Equity Capital Access Network for private investors and venture capital firms that subscribe to its funding access service.

Equity and Venture Capital Sources

Traditional banks and other lending institutions are not interested in great ideas or successful business enterprises; they only want to secure loans. Equity capital funding is very difficult for new business ventures to obtain, because traditional capitalists were inundated with requests, therefore, they could afford to pick and choose without explanation.

Small investors that are new to investing can now use an Equity Capital SourceBank as an investment option that combine with other small investors to pool their investment resources so they can invest in a much larger venture than they can alone. SourceBank combines the duties of grant providers, financial brokers and angel investors. SourceBank members are emerging class of non-accredited private investors. They are estimated to be more than 51 million people eligible to enter this new class of investors. However, the bad news for those that want to invest in early stage venture, are rapidly been price out of the market due to the acquisition range of early stage startups. The biggest problem they will face is where and how to get quality ventures to invest in. When they join a SourceBank, it will provide them with access to quality ventures and will help them to solve many of the problems they will face when competing with traditional investors, venture capitalists and hedge fund groups.

SourceBanks are easily accessible, however they will only accept applications from business owners with business model plans and third party verified business models or franchises. SourceBanks are private investment access service with exclusive rights within the Equity Capital Access Network. While the New York Stock Exchange concentrate on companies that are well established, an equity capital access company concentrated on business enterprises in the Embryonic Business Stage. Once combined, equity access capital groups will have the potential to be larger than all the present day brokerage firms listed on Wall Street combined.

The Venture Capital SourceBanks are privately operated and offer services to small business owners that need third party verified business models. They assist business owners who are seeking equity capital, instead of debt financing. They can also assist entrepreneurs with start-up ventures provided they have a written Business Model Plan.

In the past when entrepreneurs wanted a venture capitalist to consider their venture capital firms business concepts for funding, they had to send their business plans to strangers and compete with many others seeking the same funding source. This funding strategy is unlike the SourceBanks councilors that have many sources to choose from. They make equity financing available to small & medium sizes enterprises.

The Equity Capital SourceBank offer a variety of equity funding packages to small business owners, and others seeking capital to start or grow a business venture. Equity Capital SourceBanks are opening in local communities to fund certified business models they identify. The Equity Capital SourceBank may be run virtually, or can be operated out of a physical office where it can assist in the funding of certified business models and franchises.

Equity & Venture Capital SourceBanks provide investment capital access to business owners and new entrepreneurs seeking an alternative funding source. These funding sources provide both equity and venture capital instead of debt financing. They allow small business owners to locate funds to grow their business in one step instead of searching endlessly for equity or venture capital sources.

Equity & Venture Capital SourceBanks are an important part of the Equity Capital Access Network for private investors and venture capital firms who subscribe to the venture funding service they provide. The Equity Capital Access Network accepts start-up business ventures for funding long before they are ready for an Initial Public Offering (IPO).

There are two private SourceBanks attached to franchise investment exchanges, one specializes in equity investment and the other in venture capital investment projects. They were both made possible by Title III of the Job Act, a small business investment provision that allows unaccredited investors to invest in early stage startups. The new law will allow many small investors to enter the private equity market. This will cause a shortage of quality investments in Early Stage Franchising.

SourceBanks are a major part of Equity Capital Access Network for private investors and venture capital firms. Private investors and venture capital firms who subscribe to ECANN can offer access to venture funding. SourceBanks are paid a commission on the gross amount of the funds they acquire from an investor.

SourceBanks Legal Requirements

An Equity Capital SourceBank is made-up of less than 100 individuals for purpose of pooling their money to invest; members typically meet periodic to make investment decisions on early stage investment ventures, through a voting process and recording of minutes, or gather information and perform investment transactions. There is no upper or lower limit on the sum of funds invested as individuals or as a group. The Equity Capital SourceBanks is attached to ConceptStarter.Net and the Early Stage Franchise Investment Exchange and they will get first notice when business formation or investment projects become available.

Although people have been investing in groups for thousands of years, the world's first investment group was allegedly established in Texas in 1898 back in the days of the Wild West when few investments could be considered safe. Investment clubs were seen as an ideal way of spreading the risk away from just cattle. While the first investment club on record dates back to the 1800s in Western America, Various online communities devoted to this type of investing have recently emerged and have contributed to the personal investing boom in the United States. One of the reasons that people come together in investment groups is to learn how to invest.

The first step to establishing an Equity or Venture Capital SourceBank is by establishing an investment mission, policy and goals that allow active participation before investing. Consult a tax adviser on the taxation implications of the type of legal structure that fit the goals of the SourceBank. Draw up a written operating or membership agreement covering asset management rules and membership charges. These SourceBanks are often formed to purchase businesses that generate cash flow and equity. Investment types range from a group of people buying lower risk franchises with at least two years of significant revenues and positive cash flow like major fast food franchises, gas stations and hotels to higher risk businesses without an income history like start-ups, inventions, or product patenting and prototype development.

Equity & Venture Capital SourceBanks are generally formed as general partnerships, but could also be formed as limited liability companies, limited liability partnerships, corporations, or sole proprietorship that transfer assets to a group living trust (similar to a family trust). While an investment group could incorporate, the double tax treatment on corporate distributions makes the corporate structure less desirable than a partnership except in the case when a C Corporation pays out qualified dividends after deducting allowable expenses. Typically, a general partnership does not generate any tax liability on its own; instead, any tax liability is passed through to members each year. However, income taxes are generally much higher than taxes on qualified dividends.

Security & Exchange Commission
Typically, the Security & Exchange Commission (SEC) only requires reporting for investment groups with over 100 members, which is reclassified as an investment group, not an investment club. In the United States Investment partnerships must file Form 1065 and Schedule K-1s with the IRS each year, and with states that require partnership filings.

Small investors that are new to investing can use an Equity Capital SourceBank as an investment option that combine with other small investors to pool their investment resources so they can invest in a much larger venture than they can alone. The can attached to a Early Stage Franchise Investment Exchange for early stage business project in the embryonic stage of a new business idea or invest in a complete business idea. These SourceBanks are attached to a Global Cities Management Partnership or for business formation project on ConceptStarter.Net.

SourceBank Agencies
The SourceBank agencies are a privately operated referral service for small business owners and entrepreneurs with third party verified business models. The business owners they assist are seeking equity capital instead of debt financing. SourceBank Agencies is an independent brokerage they provides service for fees to private funding sources, or work directly with other venture capital firms.

Independent marketing representatives are attached to these agencies and can assist small business owners and others seeking equity financing sources for their particular business ventures.

They are paid a commission on the gross amount the business gets from an investor. The SourceBanks have a vast source of equity financing available to small business owners who enroll and need an equity capital funding source for their Micro-Business Enterprises.

Venture Capital SourceBank

Venture Capital SourceBanks provide equity funding counseling services to small business owners and entrepreneurs who want to rapidly grow their business ventures with equity financing. SourceBanks are part of a major equity capital access network for private investors and venture capital firms. Private investors and venture capital firms who subscribe to an investment scoring system provide access to venture funding. The Venture Capital SourceBanks is a privately operated venture capital referral service for small business owners and entrepreneurs with third party verified business models. Even though these source banks are easily accessible, they will only accept applications from business owners with third party verified business models or franchises.

SourceBanks also assist new entrepreneurs with start-ups and existing business owners who are seeking venture capital to expand beyond their local markets. Venture Capital SourceBank is a venture access firm with venture capital counselors attached. This is an independent investment access service that can work with private funding sources or directly with venture capital firms. Some have independent marketing representatives attached to them that specialize in a particular type of business ventures. They are usually paid a flat commission on the gross amount they raise from investors.

Venture Capital SourceBanks may provide agency services; however, they are charged an additional fee to establish them. These agents and brokers are an affiliate of the Venture Capital

SourceBank, which operates out of an executive office space with shared services for its counselors. As independent contractors they provide fees services to private funding sources, or work directly with others, such as venture capital firms.

The Venture Capital SourceBank is a privately operated referral service for small business owners and entrepreneurs with third party verified business models. The business owners they assist are seeking equity capital instead of debt financing. They can also assist entrepreneurs with start-up ventures providing they have a written Business Model Plan.

Venture Capital Counselors
SourceBanks councilors have many sources to choose from, as an independent brokerage service, they are free to work as a private funding access source or work directly with venture capital firms.

Venture capital consultants locate business owners and entrepreneurs that want equity funds to start or grow their business ventures. A private exchange for start-ups has become a reality with the increase use of an Investment Scoring System. The Investment Scoring System was developed in conjunction with angel investors, which added structure to the funding entrance level process for owners that want to acquire equity capital for their business ventures. The highest economic level a private company can reach in a free market system is to go public and sell their stock on Wall Street. Public trading stock represents the highest achievement that can be bestowed on a business venture.

Venture Capital SourceBanks are managed by Certified Venture Capital Managers. These funding access consultants provide business owners with alternative sources of financing. They are attached to the Early Stage Franchise Investment Exchange for early stage business project in the embryonic stage of a new business idea or invest in a complete business idea.

The SourceBank may be run virtually, or can be operated out of a physical office where it can assist in the funding of certified business models and franchises.

Pubic Sources of Equity Financing

The New Markets Venture Capital Program is a developmental venture capital program designed to promote economic development and the creation of wealth and job opportunities in low-income geographic areas and among individuals living in such areas. Enterprises as defined by SBA regulations that is located in Low-Income Geographic Areas. They play an active role in building investment syndicates in all of our deals, and have led these syndicates when appropriated. The syndicate partners include the very best venture firms active in the region, with each possessing particular expertise in the industries in which we have co-invested.

Small Business Investment Companies

Since 1959, Small Business Investment Companies (SBICs) have supplied equity capital, long term loans and management assistance to qualifying small businesses. The SBIC Program is one of many financial assistance programs available through the U.S. Small Business Administration. The structure of the program is unique in that SBICs are privately owned and managed investment funds, licensed and regulated by SBA, that use their own capital plus funds borrowed with an SBA guarantee to make equity and debt investments in qualifying small businesses. The U.S. Small Business Administration does not invest directly into small business through the SBIC Program.

They encourage a better understanding of their program and process for accessing SBIC capital, and keep in mind that SBIC financing is not appropriate for all types of businesses and financing needs. The Small Business Administration offers a wide variety of financial assistance programs designed to suit the varied needs of American small businesses.

Seeking SBIC Financing

Only companies defined by SBA are eligible for SBIC financing. Generally, the SBIC Program defines a company as eligible when its net worth is $18.0 million or less and its average after tax net income for the prior two years does not exceed $6.0 million. All of the company's subsidiaries, parent companies and affiliates are considered in determining the size for certain industries, alternative size standards may apply. SBICs may not invest in the following: other SBICs, finance and investment companies or finance-type leasing companies, unimproved real estate, companies with less than 51% of their assets and employees in the United States, passive or casual businesses or companies that will use the proceeds to acquire farm land. SBICs may not provide funds for a small concern whose primary business activity is deemed contrary to the public interest.

There are over 400 licensed SBICs in operation today. SBICs pursue investments in a broad range of industries, geographies and stage of investment. Some SBICs invest in a particular field or industry in which their management has expertise, while others invest more generally. Most SBICs concentrate on a particular stage of investment (i.e. start-up, expansion or turnaround) and identify a geographic area in which to focus. The form of SBA funding that a particular SBIC uses can vary and will have an impact on the type of investments they can make.

Debenture SBICs focus primarily on providing debt or debt with equity features. Debenture SBICs will typically focus on companies that are mature enough to make current interest payments on the investment so that in turn, the SBIC can meet its interest obligations to SBA. Participating Securities SBICs typically focus on making pure equity investments, but can make debt investments as well. Participating SBICs are able to invest patient equity capital in earlier stage opportunities because interest is accrued on their obligation to SBA.

Specialized Small Business Investment Companies are a type of SBIC that provide assistance solely to small businesses owned by socially or economically disadvantaged persons. Although they are not technically part of the SBIC Program, the New Markets Venture Capital Companies Program and Rural Business Investment Companies Program are modeled on the SBIC Program and may be a suitable source of capital for certain businesses.

Rural Business Investment Funds

Rural Business Investment Companies (RBICs) target investments in profit-oriented rural enterprises. The Rural Business Investment Program, which licenses and oversees joint initiatives between the U.S. Department of Agriculture (USDA) and the Small Business Administration (SBA) designed to promote economic development and job creation in rural areas.

There are extensive educational resources available to entrepreneurs that want to evaluate different risk capital options and what type may best fit their financing needs. After you have taken time to familiarize yourself with the SBIC Program, venture capital, mezzanine lending and private equity, if you believe your business would be a good fit for SBIC financing, you should first research and identify existing SBICs that may be interested in financing your company.

Some critics are understandably skeptical of the "Made in Rural America" initiative. Some critics are understandably skeptical of the "Made in Rural America" initiative. They say it promotes export of food items that the U.S. already imports in large quantity. Critics argue the initiative has also not really benefited small farmers, ag-related businesses or the consumer.

The U.S. Department of Agriculture has a $150 million fund the agency use to invest in small rural businesses. The fund establishes a new Rural Business Investment Program with a new wrinkle for investment in rural age-related companies. The new investment fund was announced as part of the Obama administration's "Made in Rural America" initiative. Agriculture Secretary Tom Vilsack said the money will go to "innovative" rural small businesses with an emphasis on those with job creating potential.

New Markets Growth Fund

New Markets Venture Partners Is A Leading Early Stage Venture Capital Firm That Invests In And Actively Assists Innovative Information Technology, Healthcare, And Education Companies. The New Markets Team Has Decades Of Experience Investing In And Building High Growth Companies, And Benefits From The Wisdom, Tenacity, And Vision Of Founders Of A Highly Successful Public Company And One Of The U.S.'S Premier Venture Firms.

The New Markets Growth Fund is a leading early stage venture capital fund in the Mid-Atlantic Region. The fund actively assists in building successful companies, and syndicates deals with the region's top venture funds. The team has a combined sixty years of investment experience, and over fifty venture backed companies.

New Markets Growth Fund prides itself on a great partner, both to its portfolio companies and co-investors. They play an active role in building investment syndicates in all deals, and have led these syndicates when appropriated. The syndicate partners include the very best venture firms active in the region, with each possessing particular expertise in the industries in which we have co-invested. The New Markets Venture Capital Program is a developmental venture capital program designed to promote economic development and the creation of wealth and job opportunities in low-income geographic areas, and among individuals living in such areas. Enterprises as defined by SBA regulations located in Low-Income Geographic Areas.

Promising companies that are located in low income areas in the Baltimore-Washington area, with its investment activities that promotes strong job growth and economic development in the urban area. These funds have the vast resources of federal, state, and university partners, including leading scientists, faculty, graduate students, and incubators, to efficiently provide its potential and actual portfolio companies with operational assistance resources, simultaneously promoting regional economic development, enhanced educational opportunities, and superior returns to its investors.

The New Markets Growth Fund is a leading early stage venture capital fund in the Maryland Atlantic Region. The fund actively assists in building successful companies, and syndicates deals with the region's top venture funds. The team has a combined sixty years of investment experience, and over fifty venture backed companies. New Markets Growth Fund prides itself on a great partner, both to its portfolio companies and co-investors.

Adena Venture Fund
Adena Ventures provides equity capital and operational assistance to high-growth businesses, primarily in Appalachia. The principals have decades of experience in venture capital, financial services, strategy, and company operations. Adena's investment focus includes growth-oriented ventures at various stages of development across a broad range of industries. From cutting-edge technology to more traditional opportunities, Adena works with portfolio companies to maximize growth.

Adena Ventures is the nation's first New Markets Venture Capital (NMVC) Company and is located at Ohio University, at Charleston. The Fund provides both investment capital and operational assistance to smaller enterprises and entrepreneurs in the Fund's target region of central Appalachia, which includes: southeastern Ohio, West Virginia, western Maryland and northeastern Kentucky. The fund is backed by twelve institutional investors, the U.S. Small Business Administration and several prominent strategic partners from both the public and private sectors, including: Ohio University of Charleston, Maple Creative, PricewaterhouseCoopers and Cornerstone Partners, Inc.

The Fund's goal is to promote shared and sustainable economic growth in the Central Appalachian region while generating market-rate returns for its investors. The Adena Venture Fund invests in diverse sectors, including information technology, healthcare and e-learning. The Fund invests between $500,000 and $2.5 million in early and growth stage companies. The Fund seeks to co-invest with other institutional investors when appropriate.

The Fund and its strategic partners also provide significant operational assistance resources to companies before, during and after investment. Examples of operational assistance services, which are provided at no cost to the portfolio concerns, include: marketing, executive recruiting, business planning, technology assessment and more. To-date, the Fund has invested in seven companies operating in diverse industries ranging from cutting-edge technology to more traditional services. The Fund has also assisted nearly fifty companies with its operational assistance program.

Delaware Valley Community Reinvestment Fund
Established 1997, Delaware Valley Community Reinvestment Fund Ventures (DVCRF Ventures) is a community development venture capital fund managed by the Reinvestment Fund. It targets existing companies in the twenty-one-county geographic region surrounding Philadelphia run by experienced entrepreneurs who have a demonstrated ability to compete profitably in their markets.

This Venture seeks to become a trusted and valued outside partner to the entrepreneur, and is committed to helping portfolio companies grow and prosper.

The venture fund will consider both equity and subordinated debt investments. The fund will typically look to exit an investment after five to seven years. This fund has assembled an outstanding team of advisors who are available to provide support, mentoring, and industry knowledge to the management teams of our portfolio companies.

Every investment venture must create quality employment in the Greater Philadelphia region in accordance with the Reinvestment Fund's mission to alleviate poverty by building assets, wealth and opportunity for low and moderate-income communities and persons. In order to ensure this, each company will sign an Employment and Training Agreement in which it commits to fill applicable job openings with qualified low-income individuals. Selected ventures can provide a link to quality job training and placement programs, thereby helping to overcome one of the key challenges to the grow
and retaining good emp

The fund looks at companies in the Greater Philadelphia region, including eastern Pennsylvania, south and central New Jersey, and the state of Delaware. It looks at companies in a wide range of industries, but is particularly interested in precision manufacturing, outsourcing services and specialty retail firms as well as health services. The Fund does not invest in tobacco, alcohol, gaming, or media related businesses. The Fund avoids companies in the seed stage and focuses on companies in the early and expansion stages that demonstrate the potential for growth and profitability.

XI. Early Stage Franchise Investment Exchange

The Early Stage Franchise Investment Exchange was established in 2012, to accommodate the large number of non-accredited investors that will enter the private equity market, after Title III of the Jobs Act is enacted. There will be an estimated 51 million new investors eligible to enter the private equity market when the law is fully implemented.

The Early Stage Franchise Investment Exchange is part of a private sector initiative that includes two access websites at: *EquityStakeExchange.Com & the FranchiseStockExchange.Com.* These websites allows the ESF Investment Exchange to be accessible from the Internet in more than 194 countries. According to industry research and the World Bank, Concept Funding generated $5.1 billion in funding transactions in 2013 and will surpass $300 billion in funding transactions by 2025.

The chance to invest in early stage startups has been all but wiped out because of the high price evaluations for new business ventures. Now even angle investors are being priced out of the startup market, while mutual and retirement fund managers are now entering the Early Stage Startup Market. It is too soon to determine how these funds will impact the growth and quality of small business enterprises over the long term.

In 2012, the Equity Capital Access Network authorized a Business Formation Period to raise seed capital from ordinary people as donor contributors. The Business Formation Period has become one of the most lucrative period in early stage investing. Early Stage Investors (ESIs) are now investing millions of dollars in the embryonic stage of a new business idea. It has been reported that these investors are investing from $1 to $10 million dollars in business ventures during this period.

Equity Capital Access Network

The Equity Capital Access Network (ECAN) provides development and support platforms for business owners and entrepreneurs that are seeking equity funding for start-ups and existing business ventures. Early Stage Investors that uses network are the first modern investors to fund the embryonic stage of a new business idea, built with business formation grants, awarded by a new class of donor contributors. These donors award business formation grants as seed money in exchange for a chance to buy into a company when and if the owner decides to sell equity stakes in their company.

The Equity Capital Access Network is a place where private business owners can showcase their business ventures to both non-accredited and high net-worth investors. ECANN.NET provides Internet access to the Equity Capital Access Network, the HUB of the Private Equity Market, for early stage start-ups. The first step for a company that enrolls in this investment access network is to get the highest investment score possible, before they contact an investor. Early stage investors do not seek funding opportunities that don't match their investment criteria. Therefore, most private investors asks for a particular scoring range when they sign-up with an Investment Access Provider maybe either an individual or a company.

The Equity Capital Access Network accept start-up business ventures for funding long before they are ready for a public offerings. High-net worth investors are joining the network to gain access to emerging growth companies. The Equity Capital Access Network is a place where business owners can showcase their business ventures to high net-worth investors with terms that are acceptable to both parties. ECANN.NET provides Internet access to the Equity Capital Access Network, the HUB of the Private Equity Market, for early stage startups.

The Equity Capital Access Network accepts start-up business ventures for funding long before they are ready for public offerings. High-net worth investors join the network to gain access to emerging growth companies.

In the past, traditional venture capitalists wanted companies that had been in business for at least seven years. Therefore, start-ups were rarely funded unless they were in high tech or biological research fields. Equity funding sources for low tech and other start-up business ventures were limited because they were not structured for equity capital financing. Today, however, all that is about to change with the introduction of new investment scoring systems and certified business models that can be converted into a franchises in months instead of years.

ECANN.NET is a one-stop shop for early stage startups that accept equity capital investments. These investments are fast becoming the favorite choice of private investors and venture capitalists. However, finding viable franchise business systems with a capable management team is a major challenge for ECANN.NET members and subscribers.

Angel investors know what industries they like to invest in and what stage of a company's growth they are looking for before investing. Today's investors even consider where the company is located and how much experience the management team has before they consider an investment opportunity. The Exchange gives enrolled business owners with high investment scores the ability to contact investors directly, that matches their investment criteria.

The ultimate, designation of a business owner with a successful venture that is built with equity capital is to become a public trading company with a listing on Wall Street in New York City. The journey begins at the owner's conception of the business enterprise and ends when the owner(s) go public on a world stock exchange. This is the goal of every venture capital firm, to find a company like Microsoft, Google or Yahoo. The highest economic level a private company can reach in a free market system is to go public and sell their stock on Wall Street. It represents the highest achievement that can be bestowed on a business venture.

The late Reginald Lewis, who built Beatrice Foods into an economic powerhouse and a billion dollar company, died before he could accomplish his goal. He didn't reach his goal of being listed on the New York Stock Exchange. However, Rudy Lewis, the author of this book was a high-school classmate of Reginald Lewis *(Dunbar High School in Baltimore)* and is the founder of the "Early Stage Franchise Investment Exchange". He is building the exchange as a wall street for early stage franchises in his honor. *(Not a relative, they only share the spelling of their last names).*

Before the ECANN.NET, there were no connections between starting a business and selling stock on a world's stock exchange. ECAN provides business growth and development platforms with business development teams attached. This allows business owners seeking funding to have access strategic partners who provide services that can enhance the owner's of raising equity capital funding. The Equity Capital Access Network provides development and support services to Franchise Stock Exchange and their investment clients.

The Equity Capital Access Network allows members to combine Early Stage Franchising with a multi-unit franchise market system; this accelerated the growth and expansion of the franchise business system being offered.

One of the major challenges of buying a multi-unit franchise territory is when you get to know the management and marketing skills of the territory development leaders that are managing the territory marketing strategy. Most master franchisees and investors meet the teams after they make the investment. Early Stage Franchising allow investors to watch them being assembled by an outside management organization.

ECANN.NET is the website entrance to the Equity Capital Access Network. The ECAN includes the following business service providers: the *Franchise Incubator Accelerator* which converts Certified Business Models into Franchises in months instead of years. The *Franchise Stock Exchange* sell complete franchise business systems, territory lease/sell agreements offer the and exclusively rights to undeveloped franchise areas too selected investors. And the *Electronic Wall Street* which showcase equity ventures seeking equity capital, using Investment Access Providers attached to the network.

Franchise Incubator Accelerator

The Franchise Incubator Accelerator shortens the time between conception and when the venture reaches the marketplace. All accepted projects begin with a Business Model Plan that is used to build a Certified Business Model that can be developed into a franchise. Certified Business Models and Franchises are built in Virtual Business Development Incubators and tested in the actual marketplace by 3rd party verifying organizations that include the National Association of Home Based Businesses (NAHBB), the Micro-Business Enterprise Association and the Early Stage Franchise Association (ESFA). These two organizations have business developers and consultants attached that can assist business owners before and after funding

The Dot-Com Business Incubator also offers comprehensive Business Model Plan Development assistance to four types of business and franchise models. The Dot-Com Business Incubator provides services that include the Business Model Plan template.

They include the General Business Model, Endorsement Business Model, and the Certified Business Model.

Business owners with Certified Business Models will get venture capital access scores that will allow them to contract investors directly. The Dot-Com Business Incubator™ includes a Business Model Plan Software that can generate Custom Business Model Plans that can be presented to financial institutions and private investors. To make business that our business model plans services are available to all the Dot-Com Business Incubator is accessible to anyone with a computer and internet access. Business developers and other support associates are attached to incubators to assist business owners and subscribers who need their services.

Equity Stake Exchange

The Equity Stake Exchange accepts business ventures in the first funding cycle. This exchange is used by investors that invest in business formation models before they become a franchise business system. This is a private equity service that concentrates on early stage start-ups. In this period an owner may choose to raise funds in the formation period of a new business venture without issuing an equity stake in their company.

Once the model is built and certified for its readiness to receive equity capital, small investors can invest in it. The Equity Stake Exchange, for early stage start-ups, recognizes business venture in the embryonic business stage of a new idea. However, they can only accept equity or venture capital for them during this period.

An equity investment is created when an investor purchases a share in a legally established business enterprise. Private investors that invest in early stage companies receive higher returns on their investments when they are sold. Early stage high-growth start-ups are less risky than traditional stocks. An equity stake is different from public trading stock and may be harder to sell or liquidate in a hurry if you need to sell. An equity stake provides direct ownership in a company where you make your investment.

Franchise Stock Exchange

The Franchise Stock Exchange (FSE) is an equity and venture capital funding platform for certified business models and franchises. The FSE accepts certified business models and franchise systems in their first and second funding cycle. Many private investors feel that this is the most lucrative period for small investors to invest. They believe that investing in a franchise business system in this select period of growth will give them a higher return on their investment.

The Franchise Stock Exchange is a key organization in the Equity Capital Access Network, with online equity capital access platforms for business owners seeking equity and venture capital for their start-ups and existing business ventures. Qualified business owners can develop a business venture in the Franchise Incubator Accelerator, finance it through the Franchise Stock Exchange, and showcase it on www.ElectronicWallStreet.Com

The Franchise Stock Exchange was established for owners with franchise business systems that need equity and/or venture capital for fast growth. The FSE assists prequalified investors that want to purchase equity capital positions with exclusive rights to franchise territories with franchise outlets. The Franchise Stock Exchange is an equity and venture funding access service for franchisors and franchisees that are expanding and need capital to grow. The FSE provides access to equity and venture capital funding for a commission or finder fee. The Franchise Stock Exchange has marketing agents attached that assist clients that are seeking capital. Certified business and franchise models make-up the majority of the franchise business systems, the Franchise Stock Exchange accepts that are seeking funding.

The Franchise Stock Exchange was established to provide equity capital access to business owners with certified business models and franchises. The Franchise Stock Exchange is also a venture capital access brokerage service for business owners with new and existing franchise business systems. The FSE specializes in multi-unit and dual-unit franchise systems that are used to expand in both domestic and foreign markets.

The Franchise Stock Exchanges provide venture & equity capital access for owners of franchise business systems and investors that invest in them. These equity and venture capital exchanges are currently attached to some of the world's largest public exchanges in Great Britain, Canada, India and Japan and in the future the New York Stock Exchange. Small & Medium Enterprise Exchanges are being established in both developed and developing countries around the world.

Franchise Opportunity Network
The Franchise Opportunity Network operates out of the ECANN.NET using its bulletin boards, classifieds and investor databases. Global Investors have arrived on the Internet investment scene and they are expressing their preference for highly organized business ventures. Therefore, tomorrow investment decisions will be based solely on how well a new venture is projected to perform in the new global marketplace.

SME Investment Exchanges
Today, a major part of the US Economy is fueled by the private equity market. Therefore, a Private Sector Business Infrastructure must be established to services the needs of new investors and business owners that are expanding using equity and venture capital. This new type of exchange will provide the last opportunity

for ordinary people to become part of the emerging business investment class.

There are major differences between using debt financing to start a business venture, than having access to equity capital while starting and growing a business venture. In the United States most business owners who start small businesses have never learned how to use alternative funding to start and grow a business. This is a logical reason for the high failure rate for start-ups business ventures in the United States. Starting a business without access to growth capital is like getting in the ring with a prize fighter with one hand tied behind your back. New entrepreneurs that use venture capital have a greater chance to start and grow a successful business. Venture capital access represents the most important link to successful business owners who have taken their company public and sold stock on Wall Street.

Early Stage Franchising is a private sector initiative that uses special institutions to provide continues development and support the franchise business system being offered. This is a predictable business structure that allows investors to easily follow the growth of the new ventures they invest in. When an Early Stage Franchise is first launched it is assigned a business development and support team to handle the constant changes it will face when entering the global marketplace.

These SME Investment Exchanges will connect accredited and non-accredited investors to small & medium size enterprise owners that are seeking equity or venture capital. SME Investment Exchanges provide new economic opportunities for all. Equity Capital Investment is created when an investor purchases shares of a legally established business enterprise. Private investors that invest in early stage companies receive higher returns on their investments when they are sold or traded.

These exchanges will play an important role in the funding of early stage start-ups, because when small investors purchase a stake in an existing business venture or make a contribution to a business formation project they want a future return on their investments.

The Early Stage Franchise Investment Exchange was established to accommodate the large number of non-accredited investors that will enter the private equity market, after Title III of the Jobs Act is implemented. Before the new law passed in 2012, there was no private investment exchanges for early stage startups in the United States were the public could invest.

These Investment Exchanges will play an important role in the funding of early stage start-ups. The key to successful investing in early stage franchising is finding the right project to invest in, during the embryonic stage of a new business idea. The Private SME Investment Exchange is unique because it allows investors to invest in the Embryonic Business Stage.

In 2013, Concept Starter Enterprises was the first to establish a Small & Medium Enterprise Investment Exchange in the United States. In the future these Investment Exchanges will be accessible from the Internet in more than 194 countries.

The SME Investment Exchange in the United States is known as the: "Early Stage Franchise Investment Exchange". This exchange specializes in early stage franchising and is currently being implemented in major cities that have an authorized Private Sector Business Infrastructure established. This is the first time in more than 200 years; a major financial investment exchange is being built in the United States.

Domestic and foreign cities with exchanges that specialize in startups will become recession proof because of the constant cast flow these new business ventures will attract. They will grow Jobs and build manufacturing plants, warehouses as well as distribution hubs for products and service that supply franchises around the world. City centers that become successful will attract other businesses that provide assistance and support services for the franchise business systems being offered. If you need examples of how a city will become a financial investment center look no further that the cities of New York and Chicago.

The Early Stage Franchise Investment Exchange is a major part of a Private Sector Business Infrastructure that connects Small & Medium Enterprises to accredited and non-accredited investors. Early Stage Franchise Investment Exchanges are being established in major U.S. Cities to service a new breed of early stage investors. These investors invest in business ventures from the embryonic stage of a new business idea to a full franchise business system.

The Early Stage Franchise Investment Exchange also includes an affiliate membership organization that has special concept funding platforms for investors that are new to private equity investing. The key to successful investing is finding the right business projects, during the embryonic stage of a new business idea. Billionaires are now investing in early stage startups and is driving up their cost, sometimes more than 1000x percent. This is causing a shortage of quality business ventures to invest in thereby, forcing new investors to compete with angle investors and equity capital firms that have more funds to invest. Plus, this is causing new investors to turn to the Early Stage Franchise Investment Exchange to help locate quality investments for them to invest in. Early Stage Franchising provides a new business system that starts at the Embryonic Business Stage.

Equity Capital Management

In the future, there will be fewer high paying jobs for people seeking long term employment. Likewise, fixed salary positions are fast becoming a thing of the past. The Equity Capital Access Network estimates that it will need 75,000 to 100,000 equity and venture capital managers. These managers are needed to establish and maintain private sector business infrastructures in cities around the world where 5 billion people will live by 2030. The Equity Capital Market for early stage startups was made possible by a new law that is part of the Jobs Act of 2012 that made it possible for new entrepreneurs and small business owners to raise equity capital directly from the general public.

The Equity Capital Managers' Training Program began in 2008 and the first enrollee was Susan E. Bate, of Richmond, Virginia. She entered the training program it was offered by the National Association of Home Based Businesses (NAHBB). Today, Concept Starter Enterprises administrate the training course for individuals that want to become an Equity Capital Manager (ECM). Ms. Bate has remained with the Equity Capital Management Program and have witness it evolved over the years, from an equity capital access service to assisting new entrepreneurs acquire equity capital. She witness the addition of the Franchise Incubator Accelerator that converts certified business models into franchises in months instead of years. Perhaps the largest expansion of duties for managers, since the program started is the establishment of the Early Stage Franchise Investment Exchange that is currently been established and activated in major U.S. cities.

There are two types of equity capital managers authorized this training program; one is the Equity Capital Manager (ECM) and other the Venture Capital Manager (VCM). Once certified, these managers can access private funding sources needed by owners with ventures from the embryonic stage of a business idea to a franchise. Equity and venture capital managers are investment access providers for the Equity Capital Access Network. The Equity Capital Manager provides assistance to business owners with new business ideas to existing franchises.

The Equity Capital Manager's training course is a prerequisite to the enrollment in the Venture Capital Manager's Training Program which can only be applied for after two years of experience in the field as an independent access provider. The Venture Capital Manager is attached to the Franchise Stock Exchange and can assist both investors and business owners. The Venture Capital Manager is an independent professional that has exclusive rights from the network to present certified business model and franchise funding packages to investment groups inside and outside of the network.

Early Stage Franchising is being established globally to accommodate Small & Medium Enterprise Investment Exchanges. The Equity Capital Manager has the exclusive rights from the SME Investment Exchange to oversee the assembling of business models and franchise funding request packages for investment groups. They also have exclusive rights from the network to present equity capital funding packages to private investors.

Transaction Management Associations

The Early Stage Franchise Investment Exchange connects small & medium size enterprises to accredited and non-accredited investors. The Investment Exchange uses transaction management associations to screen, enroll, evaluate and classify incoming business clients and others seeking access to equity and venture capital.

Following are the three main transaction management associations:

1. Equity Capital Management Association (ECMA)
2. Early Stage Financial Membership Association (ESFMA)
3. Early Stage Investment Management Association (ESIMA)

1) *Equity Capital Management Association*

The Equity Capital Management Association (ECMA) is a facilitating organization for the Early Stage Franchise Investment Exchange. This is the largest membership organization in the transaction association network. The Mission of the Equity Capital Management Association is to serve as the facilitator between the exchange management organizations including associations. Members of ECMA work directly with the Early Stage Franchise Investment Exchange. They oversee the creation and implementation of various programs and services offered by independent and major service providers.

The ECMA is considered the most diverse group in the transaction association network. This association support range from Investment programs and services to franchise development services. For example: an Equity Capital Manager's duties include assisting members in the Business Formation Incubator and the Equity Capital SourceBank. They administrate programs and services from the Business Model Plan Writing Platform to compiling information for clients that need to convert certified business models into franchises. They also coordinate the Investment Scoring System use by business owners and investors that help with the Proof of Concept by Early Stage Investors. A Scoring Range is assigned to each new venture that is posted on the Investment Transaction Listing Board within the Early Stage Franchise Investment Exchange.

2) *Early Stage Financial Management Association*

The Mission of the Early Stage Financial Management Association (ESFMA) is to establish a Financial Transaction Management Team within the business structure of the Early Stage Franchise Investment Exchange to handle equity investments and financial services as it relates to members and affiliate organizations that are authorized to conduct business on the ESF Investment Exchange The Early Stage Financial Investment Exchange include:

Financial Transaction Investment Brokerages, Agencies and Brokers. These trading floor professionals are the only ones allowed on the electronic floor to offer equity and venture capital.

Venture capital brokers are investment access providers who can own and manage their own Investment firms. However, they are not considered to be Venture Capital Brokers until they gain access to funding sources with millions of dollars to invest. These firms maintain databases of both high net-worth private investors and as well as early stage investors. Those that qualify can administrate the Investment Scoring System, a new analysis tool used by private investors to evaluate investment opportunities before they invest.

These capital access brokers also prepare venture capital funding packages for business owners and others that are seeking equity funding. Private investors use independent firms to screen there to investment opportunities, using a predetermined investment scoring range. The Investment Access Provider uses a pre-qualified list of investors based solely on an investment score assigned investment the opportunity at the enrollment process.

In order to achieve the goals of the Investment Scoring System, the Certified Business Model Plan must be synonymous with its equity funding goals. The first step for a company that enroll in an investment access network is to get the highest investment score possible before they contact an angel investor, because most investors ask for a particular scoring range when they sign-up and don't want to be bothered with venture opportunities that don't match their investment portfolios.

These firms maintain databases of both high net-worth investors and as well as early stage investors. These capital access brokers also prepare venture capital funding packages for business owners and others. Private investors use independent firms to screen investment opportunities, using a predetermined investment scoring range. The Investment Access Provider uses a pre-qualified list of investors based solely on an investment score assigned to the investment the opportunity during the time of the enrollment process.

Investment Access Provider

Venture capital brokers are investment access providers that can own and manage their own Investment firms. However, they are not considered to be a Venture Capital Broker (VCB) until they gain access to funding sources with minimum amounts of equity or venture capital to invest. These firms maintain databases of high net-worth individual investor, groups and institutions that invest in early stage ventures. An Investment Access Provider can either be a Venture or Equity Capital Broker. They specialize in providing equity & venture capital funding access to owners of Certified Business Models and Franchises. These newly authorized professionals have been added to the Virtual Capital Investment Industry to assist in assigning points to investment opportunities for high net-worth investors.

Many private investors use independent firms to screen their investment opportunities, using a predetermined investment scoring range. The Investment Access Provider uses a pre-qualified list of investors based solely on an investment score assigned to the owner's investment opportunity during the enrollment process. The first step for a company that enrolls in an investment access network is to get the highest investment score possible before they contact the investor.

Early Stage Investors use investment access companies and firms to screen investment opportunities using a predetermined scoring range. Those that qualify can administrate the Investment Scoring System, a new analysis tool used by private investors to evaluate investment opportunities before they invest. These Capital Access

Brokers prepare venture capital funding packages for business owners and others that are seeking equity and venture capital.

Many Early Stage Investors require a scoring range for each venture they invest in. Investment scoring rages are recommend for all members that invest on the Early Stage Franchise Investment Exchange These investors ask for a particular scoring range before they sign-up for membership and don't bothered with venture opportunities that don't match their investment scoring range. In order to achieve the goals of the Investment Scoring System, the Certified Business Model Plan must be synonymous with their equity funding goals.

An Investment Access Provider can either be a Venture or Equity Capital Broker. They specialize in providing equity & venture capital funding access to owners of business models and franchises. These newly authorized professionals have been added to the venture capital industry to assist in assigning points to investment opportunities for high net-worth investors.

The Investment Access Provider uses a pre-qualified list of investors based solely on an investment score assigned investment the opportunity at the enrollment process. In order to achieve the goals of the Investment Scoring System, the Certified Business Model Plan must be synonymous with its equity funding goals. The first step for a company that enrolls in an investment access network is to get the highest investment score possible before they contact an angel investor, because most investors ask for a particular scoring range when they sign-up and don't want to be bothered with venture opportunities that don't match their investment portfolios.

A person who holds shares in a company with outstanding equity shares will profit when the company is sold or acquired. Unlike, a public trading company where the value of the stock has very little relationship to the value of the company.

3)   *Early Stage Investment Management Association*

The Mission of the Early Stage Investment Management Association (ESMIA) is to oversee programs and services which include evaluations and vetting services to incoming projects that need equity or venture capital. The ESMIA include: Investment Transaction Brokerages, Agents and Brokers. The Early Stage Investment Management Association is a membership organization within the ESF Investment Exchange business structure. ESIMA oversee mergers and acquisitions offered by the ESF Investment Exchange or its members. ESIMA membership include: early stage investment bankers, commercial banks, franchise development teams, banking support & financial service institutions including private hedge fund firms.

The Early Stage Investment Management Association has pricing authority over Global Cities Project Infrastructure Partnerships. It also appoints members to the Membership of the Transaction Management board that oversee all business activities on the three transaction management associations.

ESMIA duties include posting transaction listings on the electronic board for business formation and development projects seeking equity and venture capital.

Investment Banking Division

The Dual-Unit Franchise System is a physical outlet that is surrounded by Virtual Franchise Territories. The Dual-Unit Franchise System was first use by CondoFran® an Affordable Condominium Apartment Conversion Service. It offered two systems, one for residential and another for commercial properties.

In the strictest definition, investment banking is the raising of funds, both in debt and equity, and the division handling this is an investment bank, often it is called the "Investment Banking Division" (IBD). However, only a few small firms solely provide this service. Almost all investment banks are heavily involved in providing additional financial services for clients, such as the trading of fixed income, foreign exchange, commodity, and equity securities.

Investment banks

Investment banks also act as intermediaries in trading for clients. Investment banks differ from commercial banks, which take deposits and make commercial and retail loans. In recent years, however, the lines between the two types of structures have blurred, especially as commercial banks have offered more investment banking services. In the U.S., the Glass-Steagall Act, initially created in the wake of the Stock Market Crash of 1929, prohibited banks from both accepting deposits and underwriting securities; Glass-Steagall was repealed by the Gramm-Leach-Bliley Act in 1999. Investment banks may also differ from brokerages, which in general assist in the purchase and sale of stocks, bonds, and mutual funds. However some firms operate as both brokerages and investment banks; this includes some of the best known financial service firms in the world.

Investment banks help companies and governments and their agencies to raise money by issuing and selling securities in the highly selected market. They assist public and private corporations in raising funds in the capital markets (both equity and debt), as well as in providing strategic advisory services for mergers, acquisitions and other types of financial transactions. It is therefore acceptable to refer to both the "Investment Banking Division" and other 'front office' divisions such as "Fixed Income" as part of "investment banking," and any employee involved in either side as an "investment banker." Furthermore, one who engages in these activities in-house at a non-investment bank is also considered an investment banker. Many if not most IBD employees consider the title of Investment Banker reserved to them alone and bristle at self-referential use of this title by employees of other IB divisions, especially those engaged in other sales and trading activities.

The term more commonly used today to characterize what was traditionally termed as "investment banking" is "sell side." This is trading securities for cash or securities (i.e., facilitating transactions, market-making), or the promotion of securities (i.e. underwriting, research, etc.). The "buy side" constitutes the pension funds, mutual funds, hedge funds, and the investing public that consumes the products and services of the sell-side in order to maximize their return on investment. Many firms represent both buy and sell side of investment transactions. As with most other endeavors, financial rewards await those who through luck or skill identify great opportunities, regardless of whether they are selling or buying.

Early Stage Investment Banker
In the strictest definition, investment banking is the raising of funds, both in debt and equity. This exchange group is made-up of Early Stage Investment Bankers. However, only a few small firms solely provide this service. Almost, all investment banks are heavily involved in providing additional financial services for clients, such as the trading of fixed income, foreign exchange, commodity, and equity securities. It is therefore acceptable to refer to "Investment Bankers and employees involved in either side as an "Early Stage Investment Bankers." Furthermore, those engage in these activities in-house or non-investment bank is also considered an investment banker.

Many if not most IBD employees consider the title of Investment Banker reserved to them alone and bristle at self-referential use of this title by employees of other divisions, especially those engaged in other sales and trading activities. *(These professionals come to the exchange with the proper government license as the state and federal government agency requires.)*

The United States is one of the last countries to allow non-accredited investors to invest in private equity ventures. It has been more than 80 years, since the average Americans could invest in ground floor opportunities such as; Google and Facebook. Small & Medium Enterprise Investment Exchanges are finally coming to America.

Listing Transaction Tracker

ESIMA members include Early Stage Investment Bankers, commercial banks, franchise development teams, banking support institutions, financial service institutions and hedge fund firms. The ESF Investment Exchange's Global Cities Project Infrastructure partnership stakes. It also appoints members to the Transaction Management Board that oversee business activates of the three transactions management associations. The Electronic Listing Transaction Tracker display business formation and development projects that are listed on the Early Stage Franchise Investment Exchange that are seeking equity and/or venture capital.

The Board of Advisors from the Early Stage Financial Management Association oversee exchange postings for Private Sector Business Infrastructure stakes, franchise business systems and other projects sold on the exchange for privately held companies. A Business Formation Model – BFM is offered on the Equity Stake Exchange: as BFM – 6534566. These numbers contain the Business Trade Group (BTG) numbers and the number for the business transaction number. It is the two debts at the full number that being sold on all authorized ESF Investment Exchanges and affiliate website listing boards. The same code guide numbering system is used for selling and posting of Independent Franchise Systems that is offered on the Franchise Stock Exchange. (Example of Posting - BFM: 6534566 - $50,000)

Following are definitions for Business Transaction Projects authorized for posting on the Early Stage Franchise Investment Exchange:

Electronic Transaction Tracking Terms
Business Transaction Tracking Terms are used for posting listings on the Early Stage Franchise Investment Exchange, the Equity Stake Exchange and the Franchise Stock Exchange. All authorized business transaction projects are listed on the investment exchange while business formation projects are listed on the Equity Stake Exchange and business development projects are listed on the Franchise Stock Exchange.

There is a Board of Advisors that is assembled from the Early Stage Financial Management Association to oversee exchange postings for projects sold on the exchange for privately held companies. A Business Formation Model – BFM is offered on the Equity Stake Exchange: as BFM – 6534566. These numbers contain the Business Trade Group (BTG) numbers and the number for the business transaction number. It is the two debts at the full number that being sold on all authorized ESF Investment Exchanges and affiliate website listing boards. The same code guide numbering system is used for selling and posting of Independent Franchise Systems that is offered on the Franchise Stock Exchange. (Example of Posting - BFM: 6534566 - $50,000)

Following are brief definitions for Business Transaction Projects that are posted on Investment Exchange:

Private Sector Infrastructure – PSI
Business Development Project – BDP
Franchise Business System – FBS
Certified Business Model – CBM
Independent Franchise System – IFS
Virtual Franchise Territory - VFT
Business Development Model - BDM
Virtual Business Franchise – VBF
Business Formation Model – BFM
Global Cities Partnership – GCP
Business Formation Project – BFP
Global Cities Franchise - GCF

Private Sector Infrastructure – PSI
A Private Sector Infrastructure (PSI) stake is the price the Global Cities Management charge for a city when it becomes an official Global Cities Project. Global Cities Projects provides ordinary people with a rare opportunity to participate in global business and trade, with other enrolled cities. In today's fast paced economy, small business owners need access to business and support professionals that can help them acquire equity funding for their businesses. When a Private Sector Business Infrastructure is established in a city, Concept Funding is made available to Small & Medium size Enterprise owners that want to start and grow their business ventures.

Business Development Project – BDP
A Certified Business Model development package includes a Business Developer and pre-qualified consultants assigned by the Dot-Com Business Incubator. Members of the Business Development Team specialize in different areas of business development including the Business Model Plan writing process.

The major advantage of a team focused business development process is the attachment of business developers and consultants to the venture that can provide support before and after funding. Dot-Com Business Development Team members assist subscribers by helping them to select the services as needed. A Business Model Plan that is generated on a Business Incubator Platform can be updates for the life of the business venture even when it becomes a franchise.

A Business Model Plan generated with annual updates can last for the life of a business, even if it converted into a franchise business system. Business owners who subscribe to this level of service use a Business Trade Organization such as; the National Association of Home Based Businesses or the Micro Business Enterprise Association to provide additional assistants if the business owner needs it.

Franchise Business System – FBS
Certified Business & Franchise Models are built on growth and development platforms where a business development team is assigned to each project that is being certified. Certified Business and Franchise Models are certified by 3rd party verifying organizations that test the core concept and business structure in the actual marketplace. Individual professionals that share in the business concept and management knowledge from the beginning until the early stage enterprise is funded. Team members make themselves available to business owners when needed. The business model development teams include: lawyers, accountants, business teachers, consultants, business developers, marketing & management professionals, financial counselors and others. These professionals provide the support needed when entrepreneurs need additional assistance for such things as their business plans and writing of income forecasts.

Certified Business Model – CBM

A Certified Business Model is a business venture that has had its core concept tested in the actual marketplace by an authorized third party verifying organization. The Certified Business Model is a predictable method for growing a business that's why it's preferred by new millennium venture capitalists, private investors, banks and other financial institutions. This model building strategy requires that the owner conduct in-depth market analysis, feasibility and target market research studies about their products and services. Certified Business Models and Franchises are built in Virtual Business Development Incubators and tested in the actual marketplace by 3rd party verifying organizations that include the National Association of Home Based Businesses (NAHBB), the Micro-Business Enterprise Association (MBEA) and Early Stage Franchise Association (ESFA). These three organizations have business developers and consultants attached that can assist business owners.

Independent Franchise System – IFS

There are two distinct methods of establishing a franchise system for both single and dual-unit franchises. Although, single and multi-unit franchising offers two different methods of franchising, they both have proven to be successful. The single unit franchise represents the original franchise model where a specific business was created and depended on duplicating every function exactly, for the life of the venture. Traditionally, the franchise market expansion was based entirely on the duplication of single-unit franchises. The term cookie cutter franchise model was originated to describe this method of growth. The old franchise model success was based on the principle that the models could not be changed. The addition of dual-unit franchising has proven to be even more efficient and profitable than its predecessors. The Dual Unit Franchise System works well because it allows the developer to adapt to the changing speed of technology, including the internet. Franchise models built in this manner are usually built in a small business development incubator using a business development team. This marketing strategy provides private investors and others owners with the opportunity to buy both franchises, before they are split and sold separately.

Virtual Franchise Territory (VFT)

The Virtual Business Franchise combines the traditional franchise model with the multi-unit marketing structure which allows for the selling of both the physical and virtual franchise territory rights in the same agreement. The exchange is the exclusive provider of the Dual-Unit Franchise System for the buying, selling and leasing of developed and undeveloped territory rights exclusively through FranchiseStockExchange.Com. The selling or leasing of virtual franchise territories is handled exclusively on the Early Stage Franchise Investment Exchange by Master Franchisees that buys Multi-Unit Franchise agreements. They may also sell their virtual territory agreements without seeking permission from the Franchisor. What type of territory agreement they use is determined by government agencies that oversee franchises in a country where the franchise is registered?

Business Development Model – BDM

A well written Business Model Plan aids in the assembling of information to build a business model that can be certified. This model building strategy requires that the owner conduct in-depth market analysis, feasibility and target market research studies about their products and services. This new business planning tool enables new entrepreneurs to know their business venture better than other methods of growth. The knowledge gain while assembling information for the business model planning process will aid in developing the franchise agreement. The Business Model Plan has whole page numbers and sub-page numbers making it easy for the investors to locate key parts of the plan without reading all sections.

Virtual Business Franchise – VBF

A Virtual Business Franchise is planned from the start because 90% of its functions are preformed electronically. Unlike, the traditional franchise startup that because successfully from trial and error. Concept Starter Enterprises is the chief developer for Virtual Business Franchises in the Early Stage Franchise Association (ESFA). The association maintains the integrity of the Virtual Business Franchise and its related business models by certifying their use. This business franchise system starts as an Early Stage franchise in a Franchise Incubator Accelerator and it is developed into a full- franchise system. When an Early Stage Franchise is first launched it is assigned a business development and support team, to handle the constant changes it will face when entering the new global marketplace.

Business Formation Model – BFM

ConceptStarter.Net is a Business Formation Incubator that builds business formation models for early stage ventures seeking equity and venture capital. ConceptStarter.Net accepts business formation grants awarded as seed money in the embryonic stage of a new business idea. These grants are contributed by contributors to ventures that need a Business Formation Model to attract equity and/or venture capital when the model is complete. The owner may elect to accept equity or venture capital funding at the time the Business Formation Model is complete. However, they must seek a first round of equity or venture funding within 12 months of the official completion of the Business Formation Model. The owner must also accept complete management control over the business formation model development program for at least three funding cycle. An Early Stage Franchise Model is built on a development and support platform, so that it can be changed and updated rapidly when needed. These models are developed into two distinct stages, the first is the business model formation stage and the second is the franchise model development stage. In each market

175

where early stage franchises are sold there is a Private Sector Business Infrastructure establish to support it

Global Cities Partnership – GCP

A Global Cities Management Partnership is formed when a Private Sector Business Infrastructure established to oversee the management of the selected city. Global Cities Management uses managing partners to run the day-to-day operations of the required business support institutions. A partnership maybe company owned and/or jointly owned with other investors. These partners manage all activities in the selected City(s), including development and support programs used for private sector projects. This allows city residents and others that contribute business formation grants to buy an equity stake in project that originated in the city where the business idea originates. There is a Private Equity Capital Center located in fully activated cities. These centers are used by new and existing business owners to gain access to equity and venture capital. A branch of the Private Equity Capital Center will be made available to managing partnership.

Business Formation Project – BFP

A business owner may choose to raise funds in the formation period of a new business venture without issuing an equity stake in their company. Thanks, to a small business investment provision that was signed into law, by President Obama on April 12, 2012 that created the need for the "Donor Contributor". Donor Contributors that provider a Business Formation Grant will get first option to invest in the company, if and when the owner decides to sell an equity stake in their company. These grants are given to specific ventures in exchange for an option to buy a share in the Business Formation Project, if and when the owner is ready to accept equity capital. Once, the model is built and certified for its readiness to receive equity capital funding. A Donor Contributor that provides business formation grants is the first to be notified when the Business Formation Project they selected is ready to receive equity funding. The Donor Contributor(s) that provides the formation grants will receive an option to invest when the owner is ready to accept equity capital.

Global Cities Franchise – GCF

A Global Cities Franchise maybe company or jointly owned with other partners. The Global Cities Management uses franchisees to run the day-to-day operations and business support institutions. These franchisees manages all activities including development and support programs used for private sector business projects. There is also a Private Equity Capital Centers located in an fully activated city. These Private Equity Capital Centers are used to provide direct access to equity and venture capital investors. A branch of the Private Equity Capital Center will be made available to potential franchisees that want to operate as an independent franchise outlet in a Global Cities Franchise outlet.

Transaction Tracker Devises

Transaction Tracker Displays (TTDs) come with a real time investment data listing source of franchise and funding services. The TTD allow Early Stage Investors to keep track of their investments from the embryonic stage of a new business idea to a full service franchise. The ESF Transaction Tracker Display will allow you to use your cell phone, laptop and/or desktop to get investment and listing project updates 24/7 in real time. There are three streaming services currently available for our Investment Transaction Tracker devices which include: business formation projects, certified business & franchise models, franchise business systems and global cities projects.

The best way to learn early stage investing is to subscribe to the Early Stage Franchise Investment Exchange Listing Transaction Tracker software and data collection services. The ESF Investment Exchange Listing Transaction Tracker Software provides updates for investment purchases and selling status of private sector infrastructure stakes in cities. It also includes a free Telephone App to the business formation section that record transactions in real times.

Transaction Tracker LED Display
The LED Display can also be useful at special education and training events including classrooms. The best way to learn early stage investing is to subscribe to the Early Stage Franchise Investment Exchange services with the Listing Transaction Tracker in the United States. Portable LED Display Screens are available in all sizes and can be connected to transaction listing software services that provide wall units for offices, homes and commercial events, including trade/shows and many other events.

The ESF Transaction Tracker Display provides real time investment and new funding information on current funding listings. Transaction Tracker Devises allow early stage investors to keep track of their investments from the embryonic business stage of a business idea to a franchise system. Investors can track the progress of new listings as they appear before the owner seeks equity funding. Concept funding Private Sector Infrastructure (PSI) stakes are posted the Listing Transaction Tracker observing on a telephone app you can download free.

Transaction Tracker Display
Get your Transaction Tracker Display (TTD) with real time investment and new funding listings. The TTD allow Early Stage Investors to keep track of their early stage investments from the embryonic stage of a new business idea. The Transaction Tracker Display will allow you to use your cell phone, laptop or desktop to get investment and listing project updates 24/7 in real time. There are tree screaming services currently available for our SME Investment Transaction Tracker Devices, "Business Formation Projects, Certified Business & Franchise Models, Franchise Business Systems and Global Cities Projects.

There are portable LED Screens available that can be connected to your service and hung on walls, in offices, homes and other setting such as; trade/show and special education events. The LED Display can also be useful at special education and training events.

Telephone Application
There are three telephone applications available online: one for Business Formation Projects in the embryonic stage of a new business idea, Certified Business and Franchise Models, Franchise Business Systems and another for Global Cities Projects. The Business Formation Project Tracker is free, the Certified Business Model & Franchise Tracker is for members- only and the SME Investment Exchange Tracker comes with a monthly subscription service.

Early Stage Franchising is part of the traditional franchise industry and home to the Virtual Business Franchise, the billion dollar startup with 90% of its business function preformed electronically. Early Stage Investing is the hottest new field in private equity investment for startups. The private investment market for startups is estimated to have future growth larger than all the current public stock exchanges combined.

(For more information visit: http://EarlyFranchiseExchange.Com)

Appendix
References and Bibliography
Glossary
Index

Bibliography & References

Innovative Trade Guide for Exporting and Importing

Publishing Company – NAHBB Publishing – Baltimore Maryland

Home Occupational Handbook for Home-Based Businesses By
Kendall Hunt Publishing, Advertising Entrepreneurs,

Author Marc J. Larry, John Wiley, Son Inc. of New York
Legal Guide for Starting & Running a Small Business, by Attorney
Fred S. Published by Nolo Press, Berkley, CA

Engine of Growth; Manufacturing Industries in the, U.S.
Department Of Commerce.

Article by, Susan Cantrell, the "Five Business Model Myths".
Published by the Accenture Institute of Strategic Change
USA Today Newspaper, on-line edition, article by Jim Hopkins

Technomic, a research and consulting firm servicing

James Flannigan, business columnist for The New York Times, The
Los Angeles Times and other publications, has covered national
and international business and economics for 44 years.©
Copyright 2007 The New York Times Company

Mezzanine Capital Financing for Small and Midsize Businesses,"
written by Donald Tyson, PNC Bank.By Robert Weisman, Globe
Staff March 20, 2007

The Handbook of Financing Growth: Strategies and Capital
Structure by Kenneth H. Marks, Larry E. Robbins, Gonzalo
Fernandez, John P. Funkhouser.

Canadian Investment Manager designation from the Canadian Securities Institute. Encyclopedia of Small Business

USA Today Newspaper, on-line edition, article by Jim Hopkins

CONNECT of the University of California (UC) San Diego, Since 1985

Papa John's, the first national pizza chain

Pasadena Angels, Inc. 2400 North Lincoln Avenue, Altadena

Ricardo Geromel, September, 2012 issue of Forbes Magazine

Globe Newswire, San Diego, CA - EquityNet Newsletter, 2014, by Judd Hollas

CNNMoney (New York) March, 2015

Article in April, 2015 Reuters of Shanghai

Washington post Newspaper, Washington DC., WP Company LLC

The New York Times Company Corporate Communication

The Associated Press, 450 West 33rd Street, New York, NY 100

Glossary

AdverMailer Advertiser – is a multi-insert mailer that targets residential households and commercial businesses.

American Stock Exchange – was one of the United States main stock exchange until 2008, when the NYSE Euronext announced it would acquire the AMEX.

Antitrust law – is a combination of federal and state laws which regulates the conduct and corporations assure the promotion fair competition for the benefit of consumers. This law seeks to curtail monopolistic powers within a market.

Asset – is a possession of value, usually measured in terms of money.

Billennial Generation – is a new term used to describe entrepreneurial focused children born after the year 2000.

Bond – is a certificate reflecting a firm's promise to pay the holder a periodic interest payment until the date of maturity and a fixed sum of money on the designated mature date.

Budget deficit – is the amount each year by which government spending is greater than its income.

Budget surplus – is the amount each year by which government income exceeds its spending?

Business Development Team – consists of marketing consultants, management consultants, lawyers, accountants, business developers, and many others public and private professionals.

Business Formation Grants – are contributed as seed funds for startups to develop a prototype of the product and/or service that can generate sufficient investor interest for financing.

Business Formation Incubator – is a special development system that develops a business venture from the embryonic stage of new business ideas to a Formation Business Model.

Business Model – is a business venture that includes the combination of the content of the Business Model Plan, marketing plan and growth strategy.

Business Model Plan – combines the business and marketing plans to guide the owner's from concept to a Certified Business Model that used primarily for venture capital funding.

Business Plan – is a outline and guide for a business seeking debt financing.

Business Marketing Circle – is a diversified business marketing organization for member offering a one-of-a-kind product or service.

Business Trade Group: A business trade classification that categories businesses with similar business ventures, both nationally and internationally.

Business Trade Organization (BTO) – is a private business organization that is made-up of business ventures from the same business trade group.

Bull market – is an investment market in which there is a continuous rise in stock

Capitalism – is an economic system in which the means of production are privately owned and controlled by competition and the profit motive.

Certified Business Developer – is a new professional class of consultants that have been granted a certification from an authorized business association.

Certified International Trader – is an independent exporter and importer that have been awarded a certificate of completion by the International Traders Network. This is an innovative trader designation that allows the individual to export and import from the market perspective.

Concept Funding – is used to describe; crowd funding donations, business formation grants, equity and venture capital. Concept Funding is also capital raised during the early stage growth of a new business venture.

Corporation – is a public or private venture that can offer stocks. It is treated as a private individual for tax purposes.

Crowd Funding – is financing by a group of people who pool their resources, to support projects initiated by others, including; disaster relief, writing and music production projects etc.

Custom Flash Ad – is a digital produced video ads that is less than 60 second in duration.

Market Demand – is the total quantity of goods and services consumers is willing and able to buy at prices during a stated period of time.

Depression – is severe decline in general economic activity in terms of magnitude and/or length.

Deposit insurance – is U.S. government backing of bank deposits up to a certain amount – (U.S. is currently $100,000).

Deregulation – is the lifting of government controls over a product or industry.

Direct Market Mailer – is a multi inserted print mailing that is send by postage to homes or businesses.

Discount rate – is the interest rate paid by commercial banks to borrow from Federal Reserve Banks.

Diversified Business Organization (DBO) – is a private organization that is made-up of a diverse group of business organizations

Dividend – is money earned on stock holdings; usually a share of profits paid in proportion to the share of ownership.

Dot-Com Business Incubator – is a business development system that offers comprehensive business development services to four types of business and franchise models.

Dot-Com Era – is a period in time between the 80s and 90s, where high-tech products and services were the rage on Wall Street.

Dow Jones Industrial Average – is a stock price index, based on thirty prominent stocks, that is a commonly used indicator of general trends in the prices of stocks and bonds in the United States.

Dual Unit Franchise System – is a franchise agreement that grant the franchisee the rights to own two or more franchise outlets in a designated area.

Dumping – is the sales or merchandise exported to a country at "less than fair market value, sometime below the cost to make the item.

Early Stage Franchising – is the formation period of the franchise development cycle.

Early Stage Investor – is a new type of investor that uses the proof of concept to guide their investment decision.

ECANN.NET – is an online entrance to the Equity Capital Access Network

Economic and Trade Ultra-Superpower – is a virtual nation in the western hemisphere with a combined population of more than one billion and a Gross Domestic Product (GDP) in access of fifteen trillion dollars.

Electronic commerce – is business conducted via the World Wide Web or other direct connected system such as cable.

Electronic Wall Street – is located on the Internet and showcase business formation and investment projects.

Embryonic Business Stage – is a new business venture that is recognized by experienced business developers and consultants before it reaches the actual marketplace.

Equity Capital – is the funding of a venture in exchange for a stake in a company.

Equity Capital Access Network – is a place where business owners showcase their business ventures to accredited and non-accredited investors.

Equity Capital Industry – was first organized in the 1960s as limited partnerships for private equity investments ran by professional fund managers as general partners with investors who put up the capital as passive limited partners.

Equity Capital Manager – is an Investment Access Provider for early stage startups and independent franchises.

Equity Capital SourceBank – is a one-stop equity funding source small investors seeking investment opportunities and business owners seeking equity capital for their business ventures.

Equity Stake Exchange – is a business formation funding platforms for early stage start-ups with a model. It accepts business ventures during their first funding cycle.

Exchange rate – is the rate, or price, at which one country's currency is exchanged for the currency of another country.

Exports – are goods and services that are produced domestically and sold to buyers in another country.

Exporters Incubator of America – is a training institution for innovative traders. It offers a twelve-week training program for individuals that want to become certified and attached to an innovative trader's program.

Export subsidy – is a lump sum given by the government for the purpose of promoting an enterprise considered beneficial to the public welfare?

Fast track – are procedures enacted by the U.S. Congress under which it votes within a fixed period on legislation submitted by the president to approve and implement U.S. international trade agreements.

FastTrack Business Development Program – is a small business development program that connects micro-enterprise owners to the global marketplace. It also lets business owners with business ventures that are third party verified use a private business and trade network.

Federal Trade Commission (FTC) – is a federal agency that oversees the US communications industry.

Franchising – is a business format process, which allows the owner to develop and sell their core concept and the method by which they conduct business to others for a fee and annual royalties.

Franchise Opportunity Network – is a private franchise marketing service that sells from both the Internet and through regular business opportunity channels.

Franchise Stock Exchange – is a private equity & venture capital platform for franchise businesses. It was established for owners that are seeking venture capital to grow.

Free Enterprise System – is an economic system characterized by private ownership of property and productive resources, the profit motive to stimulate production. It uses competition to ensure efficiency and the forces of supply and demand to direct production and distribution of goods and services.

Free Trade Area of the Americas (FTAA) – is a western hemisphere proposed free trade agreement between thirty-four independent countries. When fully implemented it would remove all tariffs and trade barriers between member countries, thereby creating a single market that will stretch from the top of Canada to the tip of Argentina.

Free trade – is the absence of tariffs and regulations designed to curtail or prevent trade among nations.

General Business Model – is a business structure that is built and developed by the owner of an enterprise. However, unlike the Certified Business Model it is not third party verified.

Global Cities Project – is a private business development system that was founded in the early 90s to connect major U.S. cities with large African American Communities.

Gross Domestic Product (GDP) – is the total value of a nation's output, income, or expenditure produced within physical boundaries.

Growth and Expansion Platform – is an ongoing support process that allows the owner of a business model to get assistance from a business development team when needed while the enterprise is still growing.

Home-based Businesses – are business ventures that are managed from home.

Home Business Identity Classifications (HBCI) – is a classification system that categories similar home managed businesses. They also use this code guide numbering system to identify each.

Human capital – is the health, strength, education, training, and skills that people bring to their jobs.

Imports – is goods or service that are produced in another country and sold domestically.

Industry Driven Model – is a business enterprise that is built by targeting a business field and developed on a platform which allows it to constantly change and be updated in real time.

Inflation – is a rate of increase in the general price level of all goods and services.

IntraNet HomeSite System – is an Internet marketing company that provides members with niche marketing leads.

IntraNet Marketing System – is a private Internet based business marketing service.

IntraNet-TV Broadcasting Company – is the partner company of INBC-TV.COM and HBB-TV.COM and home of niche market television.

IntraNet-TV Broadcasting Network – is a private Internet broadcasting system that represents video production, broadcasting and talent management.

IntraNet-TV Webchannel – is a private broadcast outlet for an assigned Webstation that services a particular client base with broadcast quality videos.

IntraNet-TV Webstation – is a private broadcast system with Webchannel outlets attached.

Intellectual property – is ownership, as evidenced by patents, trademarks, and copyrights, conferring the right to possess, use, or dispose of products created by human ingenuity.

Initial Public Offering (IPO) – is the first time a company offers shares of its stock to the public.

Investment – is the purchase of a security, such as a stock or bond.

Investment Access Provider – is a Venture Capital Broker who specializes in funding certified business models and franchises. Many owned and manage their own private investment access firms.

Investment Participation Level – is an option to buy an equity share in a new company when it is ready to accept equity capital.

Investment Scoring System – is a rating system that measure tangible and intangible assets; such as customer acceptance, market potential, competitive advantage, market size, niche markets, intelligent property and management team experiences.

Labor force – is the measurement of the total number of people employed or looking for work.

Laissez-faire – is a French phrase meaning "leave alone." In economics and politics, a doctrine that the economic system functions best when there is no interference by government.

Leveraged buyouts – is when another company acquisition a company using a significant amount of borrowed money (bonds or loans) to meet the cost of acquisition. The purpose of leveraged buyouts is to allow companies to make large acquisitions without having to commit a lot of capital.

Limited Liability Corporation (LLC) – is a corporation that the limit the liability of the owners and allows them to pay taxes only on the profit they make.

Market – is the setting in which buyers and sellers establish prices for goods or services.

Market economy – the national economy of a country that relies on market forces to determine levels of production, consumption, investment, and savings without government intervention.

Micro-Business Enterprise Association – is the sanctioning organization for all Micro-Business Enterprises.

Micro-Business Enterprise Institute – is a training institution for individuals and entrepreneurs that want to become teachers and consultants.

Micro-Business Enterprises – is a business ventures with fewer than 25 employees and/or annual gross revenues under 2 million dollars.

MicroBusinesses – is a niche market venture or a subfield enterprise, with no employees.

Micro-Business Trade Classifications – is an assigned code guide numbers to business venture that belong to authorized business trade groups.

Mixed economy – is an economic system in which both the government and private enterprise play important roles with regard to production, consumption, investment, and savings.

Money supply – is the amount of money (coins, paper currency, and checking accounts) that is in circulation in an economy.

Monopoly – is the sole seller of a good or service in a market with no computer.

Multi-Unit Franchise – is a unique business marketing system that allow a franchise to open more than one outlet in a designated territory.

National Association of Home Based Businesses (NAHBB) – is the leading home-managed business organization in the country. It is a membership organization that provides support and development services to members with business ventures from start-up to international trade.

New York Stock Exchange – is the world's largest exchange for trading stocks and bonds.

Niche Market Mailer – is special type of mailing that target special customer groups.

Niche Market – is a narrowly defined subfield of a major classified industry.

Niche Market Webchannel – is a webcasting system that specialize is a particular business trade group or a niche market segment.

North American Free Trade Agreement (NAFTA) – is a free trade agreement between Canada, Mexico and United States. It is being replaced in January of 2005 by the Free Trade Area of the Americas.

North American Industry Classification System (NAICS) – is replacing the Standard Industrial Classification (SIC) system in 1997, as the primary industry classifying system for industries in North America.

NuAmericas – is the name given to a new nation that is rising in the western hemisphere and it will include all the countries in the Caribbean, North, Central and South America.

Parallel Growth Strategy – is a new marketing strategy that competes directly with the multinational marketing system and will allow small business owners to establish a viable marketing alternative to the traditional marketplace.

Privatization – is the act of turning previously government-provided services over to private sector enterprises.

Private Equity Market – is a new investment market for early stage start-ups that could grow into one of largest investment markets in the world.

Productivity – is the ratio of output (goods and services) produced per unit of input (productive resources) over some period of time.

Protectionism – is the deliberate use or encouragement of restrictions on imports to enable relatively inefficient domestic producers to compete successfully with foreign producers.

QuickLink Search Engine – is a private static page search tool for IntraNet HomeSites websites.

Recession – is a significant decline in general economic activity extending over a period of time.

Regulation – is the formulation and issuance by authorized agencies of specific rules or regulations, under governing law, for the conduct and structure of a certain industry or activity.

Revenue – is the payments received by businesses from the selling goods and services.

Securities – is paper certificates (definitive securities) or electronic records (book-entry securities) evidencing ownership of equity (stocks) or debt obligations (bonds).

Securities and Exchange Commission – is an independent, nonpartisan, quasi-judicial regulatory agency with responsibility for administering the federal securities laws.

Showcase Acting Model – is a new acting field that was established to services the growing needs of IntraNet-TV.

Small Business Administration (SBA) – is a federal Agency that provides consulting, financing, support and procurement assistance.

Small Business Development Center – is an institution that is usually attached to a college and offers assistance to small business owners. These centers are authorized by the U.S. Small Business Administration..

Small Business Development Incubator – is a small business training institution that develops business models and franchises.

Small Business Network – is a private business organization management company.

Social regulation – is government-imposed restrictions designed to discourage or prohibit harmful corporate behavior (such as polluting the environment or putting workers in dangerous work situations) or to encourage behavior deemed socially desirable.

Social Security – is a U.S. government pension program that provides benefits to retirees based on their own and their employers' contributions to the program while they were working.

Standard of living – is a minimum of necessities, comforts, or luxuries considered essential to maintaining a person or group in customary or proper status or circumstances.

StarNet Portfolio Management – is an IntraNet-TV talent and casting management services for the IntraNet-TV Broadcasting Network.

Stagflation – is an economic condition of both continuing inflation and stagnant business activity.

Standard Industry Classification (SIC) – is a code guide system for industries and is used to classify manufactured products and services around the world.

Stock – is ownership shares in the assets of a corporation.

Stock exchange – is an organized market for the buying and selling of stocks and bonds.

Subsidy – is an economic benefit, direct or indirect, granted by a government to domestic producers of goods or services, often to strengthen their competitive position against foreign companies.

Tariff – is a duty levied on goods transported from one customs area to another either for protective or revenue purposes.

Trade deficit – is the amounts by which a country's merchandise exports exceed its merchandise imports.

Trade surplus – is the amounts by which a country's merchandise exports exceed its imports.

Transaction Tracker – is used on the Early Stage Franchise Investment Exchange to record and keep track of all new listing sell and new posting on the exchange.

Venture capital – is an investment in a privately owned or public enterprise.

Virtual Acting Model – is a Certified Acting Model (CAM) that specializes in electronic modeling, on websites and in video ads.

Venture Capital Firms – is a company that usually invests after the seed funding round as growth capital. Venture capital may be provided by wealthy individual investors or institutions.

Venture Capital SourceBank – is an equity funding referral service for entrepreneurs who are seeking venture capital by combining prequalified investors and business owners that are seeking venture capital to expand.

Virtual Business Franchise – is the highest form of franchising with more than 90% of its business functions preformed electronically. It also has a double level franchise territory, one for physical locations and the other for virtual locations defined by zip codes.

Virtual Business Incubator System – is a private business development service that provides assistance to entrepreneurs and others who need a comprehensive Business Model Plan to give to a potential lending institutions and equity capital funding sources.

Virtual Capital Funds – is earnings from the sell or lease of virtual franchise territories

Virtual Capital Manager – is an Investment Access Provider for business owners with certified business models or franchises

Virtual Franchise Territory – is a franchise territory that is derived from a Virtual Business Franchise that have been certified by the Early Stage Franchise Association (ESFA)

Virtual Territory Investor – is an individual or group that invests in a territory from a certified Virtual Business Franchise.

Virtual Market Mailer – is an electronic direct mail services that is delivered by email.

Urban Trading Bloc – is a worldwide business and trade system that is used by small business owners in cities.

Uniform Franchise Offering Circular (UFOC) – is document that is prepared by the franchisor and must be presented to the buyer before a franchise purchase is made.

Index

A

Amazon 89
Angel Investor 81, 84, 85, 91, 126, 151, 163

B

Bate, Susan N. 160
Billion Dollar Startup 12, 101, 123
Buffett, Warren 12,
Burger King 22, 85
Business Formation Grant 27, 30, 32, 33, 43, 98, 176
Business Formation Incubator 15, 23, 24, 75
Business Formation Model 13, 24, 25, 27, 32, 44, 121, 130, 131, 134, 141, 153, 170, 174, 175
Business Formation Platform 23, 121
Business Formation Project 33, 131, 176, 179,
Business Marketing Circle 115
Business ModelFran 59, 61, 62, 70
Business Model Plan 29, 30, 59, 60, 61, 64, 65, 66, 67, 68, 70, 74, 90
Business Trade Group 18, 19, 42, 43, 71, 79, 114, 115, 169
Business Trade Organization 82, 115

C

Canada 56, 156
Carnegie, Andrew 47
Certified Business Model 37, 66, 67, 68, 69, 71, 73, 82, 83, 90, 110, 114, 115, 121, 127, 153, 154, 170, 173, 179
China
Concept Funding 11, 12, 23, 26, 27, 36, 45, 98, 113, 158, 175
Concept Starter Enterprises 10, 23, 30, 31, 98, 113, 158, 175

F

Facebook
Financing Service Brokerage 51, 52, 55
Franchise Business Model 13, 17
Franchise Business System 14, 23, 38, 179
Franchise Incubator Accelerator 10, 13, 15, 16, 17, 18, 19, 20, 26, 29, 73, 74, 81, 86, 90, 92, 95, 98, 134, 153, 155, 175
Franchise Opportunity Network 80, 156
Franchise Stock Exchange 33, 89, 93, 106, 134, 152, 153, 155, 156, 161, 169, 170
FRANdata 104
Free Enterprise System

G

Glass- Steagall Act 54, 167
Global Cities Management 111, 167, 177
GlobalConceptStarter.Net
Globalization of Franchising 13
Global Marketplace
Goldman Sachs 55
Google 88, 152

H

Harriman E. H. 48
Hedge Fund 55, 56
Home Business Identity Classification 71, 91

I

India
Indiegogo 34
Industry Driven Model 87, 88
Infinity Marketing System 71
Initial Public Offering (IPO) 81, 123, 137
Investment Banker 53, 54, 167, 168
Investment Access Provider 126, 130, 163, 164, 165
Investment Scoring System 67, 81, 85, 126, 127, 141, 163, 164
Investment Trend Line 124

J

Japan 109, 111, 120, 156, 158
Job Act 33, 75, 98, 118, 137, 149

K

Kickstarter 34, 35, 36
Kuhn, Abraham 47

L

Lawn CareFran
Lewis, Reginald 152
Lewis, Rudy 104, 152
Lehman Brothers 77
Listing Transaction Tracker 169, 177, 178
Loeb, Solomon 47

M

Master Franchisee 11, 14, 96, 97, 99, 100, 104, 174
McDonald 22, 82, 85

N

O

P

R

Rockefeller, Laurence S. 48, 49,

S

Salz, Furman 51
Silicon Valley 46
Small and Medium Enterprises 109, 110, 112, 156
U.S. Small Business Administration 40, 113, 117, 119, 122, 142
Small Business Network 79, 121
Small Business Investment Company 117, 119, 144, 143
Start-up American Initiative 117, 118
Software Writing Platform
SolarFran Energy

T

Telephone Application
Transaction Tracker
Transaction Management Association 161

U

Union Pacific Railroad 47
United Nation
United States 28, 38, 48, 104, 105, 106, 109, 111, 113, 117, 173, 157, 158, 169
United States Steel 47, 48, 56, 119, 122, 133, 138

V

Venture Capital Firms 50
Venture Capital SourceBank 93, 136, 140, 141
Virtual Assembly Line 113

www.ingramcontent.com/pod-product-compliance
Lightning Source LLC
Chambersburg PA
CBHW081522220326
41598CB00036B/6299